NEVERTHELESS

AMERICAN METHODISTS AND WOMEN'S RIGHTS

Ashley Boggan

Abingdon Press™
Nashville

Nevertheless: American Methodists and Women's Rights

To the Methodist women in my life
who, nevertheless, preach in their own ways:

My grandmother, Nedgie Boggan
My mother, Rebecca Boggan
My sister, Emily Wineland

CONTENTS

INTRODUCTION TO A MOVEMENT

> If any one group can be said to have begun the movement of women into the larger world in the nineteenth century, it was churchwomen. They started it—moved by compassion and an ambition for a better world. . . . The beginning was made in the last century for women to cease repressing their potentialities with a myth whose basis is at best tenuous and whole biblical basis is nearly nonexistent.
> —Elaine Magalis, *Conduct Becoming to a Woman*

Men have long silenced women who speak in the public sphere with any power or authority, especially the sphere of religion. In 2017, Senator Elizabeth Warren, a self-identified United Methodist woman, spoke from the floor of the United States Senate against the nomination of then senator Jeff Sessions to the position of attorney general of the United States. During her speech, Senate majority leader Mitch McConnell invoked a rare and largely unused rule: that one senator cannot disparage another from the Senate floor. Senator Warren was reading a letter from Coretta Scott King that detailed the racist remarks, actions, and rulings that Senator Sessions had made in the past. Seeking to quiet her, Senator McConnell attempted to justify his ruling by stating, "Senator Warren was giving a lengthy speech

. . . She had appeared to violate the rule. She was warned. She was given an explanation. Nevertheless, she persisted."[1]

Nevertheless, she persisted. That final sentence prompted a new catch-phrase for women everywhere. Senator McConnell's intention to silence Senator Warren backfired, and Senator Warren's supporters immediately took to social media to support her. They posted various photos and memes of famous women throughout history who persisted—despite being told to sit down and shut up by men. Photos of the suffragettes, of Rosa Parks, of Harriet Tubman, of Malala Yousafzai, and even of *Star Wars* icon Princess Leia were accompanied with the hashtag #NeverthelessShePersisted.[2]

In the summer of 2018, #NeverthelessShePersisted was reappropri-ated by Methodist women as #NeverthelessShePreached after two amend-ments to The United Methodist Church's constitution, which would have more overtly proclaimed women's equality, failed. At General Conference 2016, one of these constitutional amendments passed, which would have added "gender" along with ability, age, and marital status to a list of char-acteristics that United Methodist churches cannot use to bar people from membership.[3] Given the similarity of the United Methodist Constitution to the US Constitution, when the amendment passed General Conference, it had to be ratified by two-thirds of the membership of annual conferences. The amendment went before annual conferences over the next year. After all annual conferences voted, the amendment failed by a very slim majority.

Also, at General Conference 2016 the delegation passed an addition to the constitution, which called the church to recognize that women, as well as men, are made equally in the image of God.[4] This amendment origi-nally (more on that later) failed to be ratified as well. In response, United

---

1   Katie Reilly, "Why 'Nevertheless, She Persisted' Is the Theme for This Year's Wom-en's History Month," *Time*, March 1, 2018, https://time.com/5175901/elizabeth -warren-nevertheless-she-persisted-meaning/.

2   Amy B. Wang. "'Nevertheless, She Persisted' Becomes New Cry after McConnell Silences Elizabeth Warren," *Washington Post*, February 8, 2017. This attack on Sena-tor Warren had come right on the coattails of Secretary Hilary Clinton being called a "Nasty Woman" by then presidential candidate Donald J. Trump in a debate. Simi-larly, these two phrases meant to silence or demean women became rallying cries for women's triumph, to showcase how tired women were of being disparaged by men for being powerful, intellectual, and in the public-political sphere.

3   Heather Hahn, "5 Constitutional Amendments Head to Vote," UM News Service, February 8, 2017, https://www.umnews.org/en/news/5-constitutional-amendments -head-to-vote.

4   Hahn.

Methodist women began to tweet #NeverthelessShePreached in homage to Senator Warren's persistence and to women who historically and contemporarily preach despite being told that they aren't equal authorities in the eyes of the church or equal in the image of God.[5]

These public acts of misogyny are not new, especially to women who use their faith to engage the public realm. From preaching for women's rights to following a call to the ordained ministry, women have long been publicly silenced—or worse, physically abused or assaulted—by men to remind women of their supposed submission in the church, and of their presumed need to be silent in public. This book chronicles the stories and fights of some of those women who have persisted, women who, despite great odds, constant public criticism, and even violence against their bodies and their existence, have persisted to preach.

Preaching here is not confined to the pulpit, although later chapters, particularly chapter 5, will focus primarily on clergywomen. *Preaching* here is defined as women using their Methodist faith as an authority to vocally and publicly argue for basic equalities before the law, be it state, federal, or denominational law.

John Wesley and Women in Ministry

John Wesley, the founder of the Methodist movement, was raised surrounded by strong women, and this, in part, may have led to his willingness to accept women's leadership within religious circles. Susanna Wesley, John's mother, is remembered and honored as a strong-willed, public-spirited and theologically attuned woman. John's father, Samuel, was an Anglican minister, and his mother, while raised Puritan, had joined the Anglican Church. Samuel and Susanna raised their family in Epworth, England, where Samuel was stationed. Susanna was the primary caregiver and educator of their children. One of Susanna's household rules charged "that no girl be taught to work till she can read very well; [since] the putting [of] children to learn sewing before they can read perfectly is the very reason why so few women can read fit to be heard, and never to be well understood."[6] This, what we might call a proto-feminist mindset, was ingrained in her children. In addition to Wesley's two brothers, he had four (or five) older sisters. Thus, many

---

5   #NeverthelessShePreached was not a United Methodist–only hashtag; it was used ecumenically by women who had overcome odds to follow a call to preach.

6   Richard P. Heitzenrater, *Wesley and the People Called Methodist*, 2nd ed. (Nashville: Abingdon Press, 2013), 28.

historians conclude that "John's later eagerness to accept the leadership abilities of women is . . . understandable."[7]

Samuel's work and, at times, his tumultuous marriage to Susanna kept him in London for weeks at a time. Once, while he was away, Susanna, displeased with the rector left in charge of their local parish, began holding meetings in her home on Sunday evenings for prayer. This type of act, in its eighteenth-century British context, was rather controversial, as it slightly violated the Act of Toleration, which stipulated that all religious meetings must take place in registered meetinghouses (not in private homes). In a series of letters between Samuel and Susanna, we learn just how strong-willed Susanna was. She blamed Samuel for her violation of the act because he'd left the parish in the hands of an inept person. "If you do, after all, think fit to dissolve this assembly," she wrote, ". . . send me your positive command, in such full and express terms as may absolve me from all guilt and punishment for neglecting this opportunity of doing good, when you and I shall appear before the great and awful tribunal of our Lord Jesus Christ."[8] Susanna was willing to obey her husband, and ended the meetings, which she believed did more harm than good, but only if he would take the blame for it when final judgment came.

Due to Susanna's influence, it is no surprise that John endorsed women's leadership, even if he had to nuance the difference between preaching and exhorting. And it is probably no surprise that he, as his father before him, also had ambivalent relationships with strong women.

In 1755, when Wesley and his fellow Methodist leaders were considering whether or not to separate from the Church of England, Wesley presented a treatise at the Leeds Conference in March 1755. In it, Wesley argued that in early Christianity, which he believed to be the most authentic and therefore authoritative form of the faith, women preached. "Extraordinary prophets" existed in the early church, and various individuals—including deacons and women—preached "when under extraordinary inspiration."[9] As he understood it, what separated them from the "extraordinary priests" was their inability to administer the sacraments. Here, we see early on in the Methodist movement that Wesley fully believed women were allowed to speak with religious authority. However, given Wesley's context and the prevailing understanding of church history, he requested that women keep only to exhorting and not preaching.

---

7   Heitzenrater, 28.
8   Heitzenrater, 32.
9   Heitzenrater, 216–17.

We can see this distinction illustrated through the preaching of Sarah Crosby. When Methodism had established a circuit of traveling and local preachers, none of the official preachers were women. However, Wesley still acknowledged the leadership of women and allowed for them to exhort. Sarah Crosby, Sarah Ryan, and Mary Bosanquet established an orphanage and school in 1763, which served as a center for Methodist activity. Here, they led prayer services and spoke from a place of religious authority to crowds of more than two hundred men and women. Crosby recalled, "I saw it impracticable to meet all these people by way of speaking to each individual. I therefore gave out an hymn, and prayed, and told them part of what the Lord had done for myself, persuading them to flee from all sin." And she was unapologetic about her preaching, "I do not think it wrong for women to speak in public provided they speak by the Spirit of God."[10] For her actions, Sarah received a letter from Wesley in which he reminded her to not preach but also encouraged her to publicly read portions of his own sermons. He suggested this to his traveling preachers as well.

When women did preach, Wesley did not remove them from their positions. Most of the time, he simply wrote a letter reminding them to exhort, not preach—a small consequence. Given what Wesley could have done to prevent women from holding leadership positions, which brought them dangerously close to preaching, he did very little, and thus we can infer that women as preachers, especially given his mother's influence, was not the worst thing in his mind. But, in the 1760s, Methodism was still new and rather controversial in England, and to keep the Methodist movement from dissenting fully from the Church of England, he had to have a written record that he had taken some sort of corrective action.

A decade later, however, with the same women just named, there was a shift in Wesley's attitude. Bosanquet and Crosby continued their ministry within the school and orphanage. Sometimes, the meetings where they spoke were not held in the school or orphanage but in a registered preaching house, and their speaking began to look more and more like preaching. In 1771, one of the other Methodist preachers took issue with what the two women were doing and wrote to Wesley about it. Many others also joined in quoting Paul and his disapproval of women speaking, let alone preaching, within churches. Rising to their own defense, Bosanquet also wrote to Wesley a letter that historian Richard P. Heitzenrater calls "a masterful combination of biblical exegesis and spiritual mandate." In this letter, she requested that women be allowed to follow the same call to preach that men do. And

---

10 Heitzenrater, 264.

she felt called: "I do not believe every woman is called to speak publicly, no more than every man to be a Methodist preacher, yet some have an extraordinary call to it and woe be to them if they obey it not." Reading this, Wesley had little argument against it, and he was thereafter willing to accept the extraordinary call and leadership of women on a case-by-case basis. His written record and the Methodist discipline did not change, but in private and for some women, a call to preach was undeniable.[11]

Methodist Women and the Eradication of Social Sin

Since the beginning of the Methodist movement, Methodist women have sought to use their voice to eradicate what we can now call social sin. To better understand their efforts, we first need a bit of background. Methodist theologian Joerg Rieger reminds us that sin is too often limited to notions of dos and don'ts with regard to personal morality, particularly sexuality. Instead, he insists, sin has to be understood in light of "the broader biblical concern for sin in terms of oppression, injustice, and the biblical concern for the poor."[12] Systemic injustice and systemic oppression of women through a heterosexist, racist, and patriarchal association of white maleness with the divine image of God is one of the gravest and longest-lasting sins of the Christian tradition. John Wesley showed Methodists a way out of this sin, through his own admission that it was not up to him to decide whom the Holy Spirit did and did not work through. The call to ministry and the authority to preach were in the hands of God, not (literal) man. However, after Wesley's death, in an effort to become more mainstream and less countercultural, the leaders of the Methodist movement in America, particularly Rev. Francis Asbury, limited the authority of women. No longer were they allowed to openly preach—even on a case-by-case basis. Instead, seeking to gain power, prestige, and respect in society, male leaders restricted women to more "appropriate" spheres of ministry—the eradication of sin in their private households through ensuring that their husbands were moral and that their children were good Christian citizens.

Finding little satisfaction in this largely private and highly regulated role, Methodist women began to take seriously the definition of sin beyond the personal level to include societal ills, all while using Methodist theological foundations. For John Wesley, the ministry of Jesus was oriented toward

---

11 Heitzenrater, 276–77.

12 Joerg Rieger, *No Religion but Social Religion: Liberating Wesleyan Theology* (Nashville: Wesley's Foundery Books, 2018), 23.

social justice, toward a breaking down of institutional harm that prevented people from being able to live their lives to the fullest. This is perhaps best summed up in Jesus's words in John 10:10: "I came that they may have life, and have it abundantly." An abundant life is one that is not plagued by systemic oppression. It is one where people, no matter their gender identity, can seek to follow a call to ministry. Everyone should feel able to speak the truth in love from a public platform or pulpit.

The term "social justice" did not exist during Wesley's or Jesus's lifetime, but the concept did. Wesley knew that "the Gospel of Christ knows of no religion, but social; no holiness but social holiness."[13] This is a Wesleyan definition of social justice rooted in Scripture. If we are to emulate Christ, if our goal is to continuously try to be more Christlike, more reflective of the love of God in and through our lives, then we will be engaged in what Wesley called social holiness.

Social Holiness

Social holiness is the love of God lived in and through us and then reflected in the world around us. For Wesley, a true love of God could not be contained inside a person, nor could it be expressed in a solitary form, because "Christianity is essentially a social religion, and to turn it into a solitary one is to destroy it."[14] A true love of God was too overwhelming to be contained; it, therefore, had to be lived outwardly among others and toward neighbor. Furthermore, a true love of neighbor could not watch a neighbor suffer and be kept silent under systemic oppression. To avoid oppression, a true and lived love of God would work to dismantle the systems that cause oppression. Wesley called this social holiness; today, we call it social justice.

Throughout his life, Wesley continually emphasized in word, and demonstrated in action, a ministry that was social justice oriented. To deny this claim, as many try to do, is to deny his own words and actions. Wesley repeatedly left the four walls of the institutional church of his day and took the message of Jesus to those who were not welcome inside or weren't comfortable entering its walls. What made Wesley unique was his lived

13 John Wesley, preface to *Hymns and Poems* (1739) in *The Works of the Reverend John Wesley, A. M.* (New York: J. Emory and B. Waugh, for the Methodist Episcopal Church, 1831), 7:593.

14 John Wesley, "Upon Our Lord's Sermon on the Mount: IV," in Albert Outler, ed., *John Wesley's Sermons: An Anthology* (Nashville: Abingdon Press, 1991).

theology. For him, theology was practical, something that had to be lived out and practiced in everyday life. As Rieger argues:

> It is widely acknowledged that John Wesley himself was not only aware of the grave pressures of life in his time but that he was also involved in efforts to alleviate them. He did not only consider the plight of workers, the poor, the prisoners, the sick, and the slaves; he structured his societies in such a way that the plight of these groups was alleviated—not merely through service to them, but by bringing them into communities. This set him apart from professional theologians, both past and present, who may well be aware of some of these pressures but who consider them of little relevance to the discipline or even as a disturbance to their work.[15]

Wesley recognized the increasingly large economic gap of eighteenth-century England and worked to bring light to the failure of economic systems.[16] He famously called out his fellow Oxford dons for not being true scriptural Christians because they did not engage with those who were economically disadvantaged but instead ministered primarily with other privileged persons.[17] Wesley knew that education was key to a better life and built schools for orphans, for the disadvantaged, and for the privileged.[18] He also knew that slavery was an immoral and unnecessary abuse of humanity and was contrary to the liberating message of scripture.[19] He knew that health might prevent people from being able to live full lives, and even though many of his "remedies" would not pass medical protocol today, he sought to provide his followers and preachers with basic relief to common ailments.[20] Wesley visited the sick, the hospitalized, and the imprisoned. He did not care that others ridiculed him for doing so or for associating with people whom

---

15 Rieger, *No Religion but Social Religion*, 11.
16 See Wesley's *Thoughts on the Present Scarcity of Provisions* (London: R. Hawes, 1773).
17 See Wesley's 1744 sermon "Scriptural Christianity," in Outler, *John Wesley's Sermons*.
18 See Wesley's sermon "On the Education of Children" in Wesley, *The Works of the Rev. John Wesley, A.M.*, 4th ed. (London: John Mason, 1840), 7:82–93. Wesley's Kingswood School, outside of Bristol, England, was "designed to instruct children 'in every branch of useful learning,' from the alphabet to those qualifications that would fit one for 'the work of the ministry.'" Heitzenrater, *Wesley and the People Called Methodist*, 168.
19 See Wesley's *Thoughts upon Slavery* (Dublin: W. Whitestone, 1775).
20 See Wesley's *Primitive Physick: Or, An Easy and Natural Method of Curing Most Diseases* (London: R. Hawes, 1774).

society deemed "unseemly."[21] For Wesley, nothing came closer to the ministry of Jesus than communing with and loving the outcasts of this world. He believed in working for and with the grass roots. He called out the institutional church for being too bureaucratic to recognize the human hurt around it. To live out God's grace, Wesley knew that he had to move beyond the confines of the institutional church and reach out to those who needed it most.

He also knew that he was not alone in this mission, that the love of God must be spread and lived around the world by everyone, which in our day includes men, women, trans*, and nonbinary people. And who was Wesley to say who could and could not spread this message of love? Who was he to say who could and could not preach the Word and love of God? Who are *we* to say such things?

Women who stepped outside of their "place" were often labeled as sinful, as deviant, because they went against the oppressive social norms, which sought to impose limits on their public presence. They were told that because they were women, they could not be called by God to preach, they could not speak out in public or in church, and that their God-given duty was to submit to their husbands and raise responsible Christian children. Methodist women, using Wesley's theological foundations of social holiness, knew that they had to change the definition of sin in their own times in order to make a brighter and better future for the world at large.

Being Methodist emboldened women to reach beyond the social confines of their time to find political avenues of social justice. These women engaged in mission work that sought to not simply fix social ills but to prevent them from happening again. They strove to address the systemic and hegemonic causes of oppression. Those women who "stept out of their place" have been researched, and their stories are recorded by historians.[22] By joining missionary societies in the nineteenth century, Methodist women

21 There is even evidence that Wesley ministered with Mr. Blair, a man imprisoned and sentenced to death for sodomy. This is one of the few examples we have of Wesley ministering with individuals convicted of this act.

22 See Rosemary Skinner Keller, *Spirituality & Social Responsibility: Vocational Vision of Women in The United Methodist Tradition* (Nashville: Abingdon Press, 1993); Alice Knotts, *Fellowship of Love: Methodist Women Changing American Racial Attitudes, 1920–1968* (Nashville: Kingswood Books, 1996); Jean Miller Schmidt, *Grace Sufficient: A History of Women in American Methodism, 1760–1939* (Nashville: Abingdon Press, 1999); Sara M. Evans, *Journeys That Opened up the World: Women, Student Christian Movements, and Social Justice, 1955–1975* (New Brunswick, NJ: Rutgers Univ. Press, 2003); Ellen Blue, *St. Mark's and the Social Gospel: Methodist Women and Civil Rights in New Orleans, 1895–1965* (Knoxville, TN: Univ. of

set the stage for twentieth-century Methodist women to use their faith to engage more directly in politics. Historian Ellen Blue recently wrote and published an exceptional history of Methodist women engaged in mission over the last 150 years. She claims, "Through the new mission societies developed in the 1800s, large numbers of women learned leadership skills and found the courage to use them."[23] Women who participated in these early missionary societies found themselves transformed by their work: "They realized that if they wished to see social change, they would have to promote social action and were convicted by the Holy Spirit to break 'barriers of prejudice, isolation, and distrust, which keep all people from sharing in the gospel message.' This required them to move beyond the walls of the church."[24] The work of these nineteenth-century women formed the basis of the work of those in the twentieth century. Without their efforts to reach beyond the walls of the church, twentieth-century women would not have had a chance to then reach into the walls of the United States Capital.

Being a Methodist woman required creative avenues for God's mission in the world. Women were not allowed to serve in ordained ministry in the Methodist Church until 1956. But this also meant that women were not confined to ministry in the pulpit but were given the freedom to find ways of embodying God's call outside the walls of the church. Through participation in the Woman's Christian Temperance Union, the Woman's Foreign Missionary Society, the Women's Home Missionary Society, the Wesleyan Guild, and even more secular political campaigns, Methodist women found a sense of authority that allowed them to make a tangible difference in the lives of those around them and to live into their calls.

In 2008, The United Methodist Church expanded its mission statement, "to make disciples of Jesus Christ," to align it more with the social holiness of John Wesley. The United Methodist Church now seeks "to make disciples of Jesus Christ *for the transformation of the world*."[25] Some believe that this change has moved Methodists from their task of spreading scriptural Christianity across the world. However, if we actually look at Methodist history since the time of John Wesley, especially at the actions and faiths of Methodist women, we will see that transforming the world has always been front and center. Rieger argues that "there are big differences between

Tennessee Press, 2014); and Ellen Blue, *Women United for Change: 150 Years in Mission* (New York: United Methodist Women, 2019).

23 Blue, *Women United for Change*, 12.
24 Blue, 12.
25 Emphasis added.

charity, advocacy, and solidarity. While charity and advocacy are examples of valiant efforts to support others, mutual relationships cannot develop without solidarity."[26] Rieger here is talking about what it means to practice social religion or to express social holiness. It isn't simply giving money to people or nonprofit organizations. It isn't advocating for people who need it. Social religion and social holiness are about being in relationship with other people, learning from them what systemic injustices they are facing, and then working with them to fix those injustices. Rieger continues, "Christianity is not primarily about religion or morality. It is about grace that makes a difference in the world and in people's live, grace that is potently at work where we least expect it: in situations of pressure."[27] One of the things that makes Methodism unique is its emphasis on grace. For Wesley, God was, is, and always will be in us, even before we know it. This prevenient grace is there waiting for us to acknowledge and accept it. Once we've done so, we are forgiven by God's justifying grace. At the same time of this forgiveness, we are filled with an overwhelming love of God that must be expressed outwardly through sanctifying grace, the grace that Rieger emphasizes here. It is that grace that pushes us to a make a difference in the world around us and the grace that we must continually grow in if we want to bring about the kingdom of God here and now.

Rieger places John Wesley in line with contemporary liberation theologians. He claims, "What we see at work [in Wesley], therefore, is a fundamental way of doing theology, which was not invented in the 1970s but is much older." Gustavo Gutierrez is usually given credit for creating liberation theology and reminding Christianity that Jesus had a preferential option for the poor and oppressed, and thus, social justice should be the central feature of any and all Christian theologies. Gutierrez bases this preference, rightly, in the ministry of Jesus. However, Rieger argues that there are people who can be called liberation theologians who lived between the ministries of Jesus and Gutierrez and who held a preferential option for the poor and oppressed. Thus, Rieger argues that there "has never been a unilateral liberation theology" because as societies grew and changed, new pressures were born, and liberation theologies have had to "wrestle with grace in the context of particular pressures."[28] John Wesley's context gave rise to its own social pressures, to which Wesley felt a sincere, grace-led duty to respond and upend. Methodists since then, especially Methodist women, would

---

26 Rieger, *No Religion but Social Religion*, x.
27 Rieger, 1.
28 Rieger, 7–8.

continue this call to respond to social pressures through grace-led, socially engaged, and unapologetically public work.

Methodist women did not simply apologize for the sins of the society. Nor did they look for quick solutions to social sin. They did not just donate money or seek to convert souls, hoping those newly awakened souls would innately know how to act in non-sinful, non-oppressive ways. While monetary donations and conversions are important, for many Christians, they are Band-Aid fixes and will not permanently change the lives of those experiencing oppression because of systemic harm. These women sought to remedy social sin by engaging in political reform for the sake of social justice and for the transformation of the world. To create more equitable societies, where all had access to the things that would improve and better their experience of the kingdom of God here on earth, these women worked to prevent the spread of systemic social sin. They did so through education, through legislation, through speeches, through petitions, through public and pulpit witness, and through an unrelenting spirit that refused to acknowledge failure. They continued to push the boundaries of what it meant to be a woman, a Methodist, a Christian, and even an American.

Chapter Outlines

I would like to thank Ellen Blue, Alice Knotts, and Ellen Kirby for speaking with me on these topics, pointing me to rare and underutilized sources, and being fierce women preachers in their own ways. This book chronicles Methodist women's involvement and engagement with the political realm. This is not an exhaustive list by any means, but a mere sampling of Methodist women who have used their voices to preach equity. I have limited our discussion to women in America, as the focus of this text is on their involvement with American politics and American political rhetoric. The women herein are involved with Methodist agency or organizations at some level, meaning that their writings, speeches, mission work, and stories have been chronicled somewhere and are thus more readily available to the general public. There are countless Methodist women, in America and beyond, who did this type of work and whose voices were, tragically, never recorded for historians to use. Hopefully, the words of these women who were privileged enough to have stories recorded will help us realize how Methodist women worldwide have made a difference in their societies.

These religiously motivated women fought to eradicate the sins of society, providing themselves and others a more equitable place in society. Chapter 1 of this book focuses on women's efforts to have their voices heard and counted in the public realm—whether in the pulpit with ordination rights or at the ballot box with the right to suffrage. These women used religiously centered rhetoric to argue for both ordination and suffrage. The chapter will focus on two women who had very different strategies in this fight—Frances Willard, whose political genius appealed to conservative and liberal white women; and Anna Howard Shaw, who fought for ordination within the Methodist Episcopal Church and then went on to lead the National American Woman's Suffrage Association.

Chapter 2 focuses on women who preached racial equity. Divisions within the suffrage movement meant that a majority of the women prioritized white women's issues over racial equity, and the vote in 1920 was granted only to white women.[29] However, some Methodist women fought for equality of African American women. This chapter chronicles the efforts of those women who recognized that the argument that women are also made in the image of God did not apply only to those who were white. It follows the lives and ministries of Theresa Hoover and Thelma Stevens and their contributions to the Woman's Division of the Board of Missions of the Methodist Church, which traces its own roots back to the Methodist women's missionary organizations of the late nineteenth century and would later become part of the General Board of Global Missions.

Chapter 3 details Methodist women who used the rhetoric of equality in the US Constitution and equality within the image of God to argue for the passage of the Equal Rights Amendment (ERA). There is very little scholarship on how Protestant denominations were involved in the fight to pass the ERA, despite the fact that they were heavily involved in passing this amendment. This chapter does not do their fight justice, but it begins the conversation of how Methodist women fought to ratify the ERA after its passage by Congress.

Chapter 4 is a bit different. Its story does not start with Methodist women in leadership but instead with Methodist men fighting on behalf of women for their right to access a legal and safe abortion in the mid-1960s. Within a few years, however, women had taken over this effort within The United Methodist Church through their advocacy efforts in the Commission on the Status and Role of Women, United Methodist Women, and the General Board of Church and Society. These three organizations, after the

---

29 This is due in large part to literacy tests and other means of preventing African American men and women from voting, particularly in the South. These literacy tests (and other means of voter suppression) would remain in place until the passage of the Civil Rights Act and Voting Rights Act in 1964 and 1965.

passage of *Roe v. Wade*, founded the Religious Coalition for Abortion Rights, an ecumenical organization that endeavored to provide a religious voice in support of a woman's right to an abortion.

Chapter 5 brings us to today and the emergence of #MeToo. The United Methodist Church has taken great strides to end sexual misconduct, harassment, and abuse within the denomination. However, its efforts have historically focused on the harassment of female congregants by clergymen—a necessary but limited focus. This chapter is partially reliant on Rev. Dr. Beth Cooper's research of the harassment of clergywomen by laymen and situates this research within the larger conversation of #MeToo and #ChurchToo and the problem female clergy face because of the stained-glass ceiling.

The conclusion will bring the previous chapters in line with the most contemporary acts of Methodist women engaging voting rights, racial equity, gender equality, abortion access, and defense against sexual harassment. There is not enough room in the confines of these pages to exemplify the work of all Methodist women who have engaged in this type of work. Nor is there room to address all of the systemic sins that plague our world. The purpose of this book is not to be a complete overview of Methodist women in social justice reform. Thus, systemic sins addressed will be limited to twentieth- and twenty-first-century America. The purpose of this book is to bring to light a few examples of women working to prevent social and systemic sin from recurring through the use of their voices as women of faith. It is meant to help Methodists—women and men, as well as non-Methodists—reflect on their own roles in political engagement and how their faith informs their social engagement in this world. It is meant as a celebration of those who came before us and those who continue this work today and an inspiration to engage this work in the future.

ONE: SUFFRAGE

> Last night someone asked, "What shall we do with a woman who says
> she has all the rights she wants?" The answer came to me in a flash and
> I said, "Give her another and see how quick she will take it.'"
> —Anna Howard Shaw, in a letter to Lucy E. Anthony, 1897

> This is what life is for—To *be* & to *do good*. Whatever I forget, may I
> remember this.
> —Frances Willard, 1866

The right to vote has been a primary concern for white women since the
1840s. White Methodist women joined in this effort primarily through social
reform organizations. Using the tactics they had learned through female missionary organizations, Methodist women stepped out into the world to bring
about Wesley's social holiness. The best way to do that was ensuring that
white women had access to the ballot box. By the end of the nineteenth
century, Methodist women were moving beyond missionary organizations
toward organizations that focused more on social and political reform here in
the United States. Two of the presidents of those organizations will be high-
lighted in this chapter. One of the first women to be ordained in the Methodist tradition (via the Methodist Protestant Church), Rev. Anna Howard Shaw,

was an early advocate of women's rights, both within the church and in American politics. Another Methodist woman who advocated strongly for women's rights, through her tenure as president of the Woman's Christian Temperance Union, was Frances Willard. An influencer of Shaw, Willard was a few years older than Shaw. These two women exemplify how Methodist women used their Wesleyan heritage to argue for women's empowerment, specifically their right to voice their authority from the pulpit or the ballot box.

Willard and Shaw were both raised in the Midwest and converted to the Methodist faith for spiritual and professional reasons. Both were presidents of major national women's associations of the late nineteenth and early twentieth centuries—Willard the Woman's Christian Temperance Union and Shaw the National American Woman's Suffrage Association—organizations whose memberships multiplied many times over under their leadership.[1] Their lives, ministries, voices, and calls for social justice will be outlined throughout this chapter to illustrate how Methodist women, empowered by a love of God and neighbor, asserted themselves and their voices in the politics of their day.

Frances Willard

Frances Willard is probably one of the more well-known Methodist lay-women. Born in western New York and raised in Wisconsin, Willard was reared in a "carefree country existence" by a temperance-minded family with a mother who encouraged daily journaling.[2] She received a formal education at North Western Female College in Evanston, Illinois, and after graduation in 1859, she taught for ten years. By 1871, she had advanced her teaching career to become the president of Evanston College for Ladies. When Evanston College merged with Northwestern University, she became the first female dean of the women's division of a coeducational college. However, after disagreements with the administration (her former fiancé was head of Northwestern during her tenure), she left education to join a movement that she knew all too well—the temperance crusade.

This was a new women's organization making its way across the nation, joining women together who sought temperance reform—the Woman's Christian Temperance Union (WCTU). By 1874, Willard was president of

---

1   The WCTU under Willard would become the largest women's organization in the US, with just under 150,000 members.

2   Carolyn De Swarte Gifford, ed., *Writing Out My Heart: Selections from the Journal of Frances E. Willard, 1855–96* (Chicago: Univ. of Illinois Press, 1995), 5.

the Chicago Woman's Christian Temperance Union, a regional body of the national organization. At the first national convention of the WCTU in 1874, Willard was elected its corresponding secretary, a position that honed her organizational and rhetorical skills. By 1879, she was elected president of the WCTU and served until her death in 1898.[3] It was while serving as president that Willard's Methodist faith encouraged her to push the WCTU's female membership to "Do Everything" to eradicate social and systemic sin.[4] For Willard, the social sin was alcohol, and the systemic sin was the lack of women's voices from the pulpit and the ballot box.

Willard was introduced to Methodism through her education at various Methodist institutions. She began her conversion to the Methodist faith in 1860 at age twenty-one by joining the Evanston Methodist Episcopal Church. She would soon rise to become one of the "most prominent laywom[e]n" in Methodist history. Willard's Methodist community was a tight-knit one. Its "main settings—Evanston's Methodist Church, NU [Northwestern University], GBI [Garrett Bible Institute], and NWFC [North Western Female College]" were all Methodists institutions and were "within walking distance of each other." Willard knew members of all of these institutions, for these "friends, neighbors, and teachers" whom she "greeted at Sunday morning worship" were also seen "throughout the week in a round of events that had as their primary purpose the strengthening of Christian character." This Evanston-based Methodist community was "a powerful community of intellectual, moral, and religious striving" that recognized Willard as a devout and power-ful figure of Methodism.[5]

One of her many biographers, Ruth Bordin, claims, "Her affection for the Methodist church was both deep and genuine. . . . Although her causes varied, her style was Methodist to the core. The enthusiasm of enthusiastic religion and John Wesley's method and rule as applied to social concerns were at the very heart of the way she worked."[6] Here, enthusiasm means that overwhelming power of love that cannot be contained within a person. In early Methodism, this enthusiasm was best expressed through shouting and dancing and led to Methodists being nicknamed "shouting Methodists." In Willard's day, after the fight for abolition and in the midst of increased industrialization, urbanization, and the beginnings of the Social Gospel

---

3   Gifford, 6.
4   Gifford, 366.
5   Gifford, 11.
6   Ruth Bordin, *Frances Willard: A Biography* (Chapel Hill: Univ. of North Carolina Press, 1986), 155.

movement, Methodist enthusiasm was expressed as social reform. Willard's social reform focused on the rights and status of white women both within her Methodist denomination and within the country at large.

Within Methodism, Willard fought to give white women a voice at the table and from the pulpit. In May 1880, she attempted to address the General Conference of the Methodist Episcopal Church, one of the first women to ever ask to speak at this quadrennial legislative gathering of Methodist clergy and laymen.[7] She attended on behalf of the WCTU, trying to strengthen the relationships between the organization and various Protestant bodies. Even today, in order to speak at The United Methodist Church General Conference, one either has to be a seated delegate (who in Willard's day were only male) or invited to speak by a majority vote of the seated delegates. Rather quickly in 1880, "Willard recognize[d] how deep was the feeling of the Methodist hierarchy against the participation of women in the governance of the church." Upon her request to speak, a debate broke out on the floor of General Conference. Willard recalled, "As the acrimonious debate dragged on, it became clear that the General Conference was really addressing itself to the 'Woman Question.'"[8]

The "Woman Question" refers to the latter half of the nineteenth century's debate on women's place in the world. Driven primarily by a political rhetoric that historians call first-wave feminism, it was the desire and efforts of women to seek equality before the law. The Woman Question applied to all women, but first-wave feminists have, justifiably, been critiqued by modern-day historians and feminists as racist for their overt attempt to silence African American women and to limit African American women's claims of equality based on white supremacist notions of white women's superiority and their unique equality to white men, all of which can be seen in Willard's own beliefs.[9]

Willard's main opponent at the Methodist Episcopal Church's General Conference was Rev. James M. Buckley, a clergyman from Brooklyn, New York, and editor of the *Christian Advocate*, who feared that allowing a woman

7   The General Conference of the MEC first included laymen in their proceedings in 1872. The MEC South included laymen earlier, 1866. Women were not allowed to be seated as laywomen until 1904 in MEC and 1922 in MEC South. For more see Russell Richey, *The Methodist Experience in America: A History*, vol. 1 (Nashville: Abingdon Press, 2010).

8   Bordin, *Frances Willard*, 160-161.

9   Louise Rachel Newman, *White Women's Rights: The Racial Origins of Feminism in the United States* (New York: Oxford Univ. Press, 1999).

to speak to General Conference would set a "dangerous precedent."[10] Despite his best effort, Willard was invited to speak to the floor of General Conference by a vote of 238 to 138. However, afraid that speaking would harm the relationship between the denomination and the WCTU, Willard declined the invitation after her supporters advised her to.

This experience led Willard to be increasingly critical of the institutional church. Those who had questioned her ability to speak before men at the 1880 General Conference were her friends, colleagues, and those who had frequently taken advantage of her rhetorical skills when it had suited them and their efforts. Their blatant hypocrisy led Willard to conclude that Protestant churchmen took advantage of her and other women when it benefited them but were quick to resist women's leadership and abilities when they began to exert any sort of independence or power. To combat this, she wrote *Woman in the Pulpit*, which unapologetically argued that women had an equal standing with men and should be allowed ordination.[11]

Willard continued her campaign to fight for a woman's voice within the MEC, and in 1887 she was elected as a lay delegate from the Rock River Annual Conference to the 1888 General Conference of the MEC. She was one of five women, all from different annual conferences, elected as lay delegates for 1888. Their election received national press, covered by denominational press and the *New York Times*. Willard, unable to attend due to her mother's failing health, advised her surrogate, Anna Gordon, and the other four women to be strategic and make "substitute motions, second amendments, another phraseology, and a reminder to male lay delegates that it was women's votes that had brought them their seats in the Conference."[12] The male seated delegates refused to seat the elected female delegates on the floor of General Conference, despite their best efforts and their legitimate election. Angered and hurt by this defeat, Willard and the WCTU strategized for the 1892 General Conference: "The *Union Signal* advised women to inform their hometown ministers of the arguments for admitting women to the Conference, and *Woman in the Pulpit* was available to give them ammunition and reason. The church press countered by accusing Willard of consorting with doctrinal heretics."[13] Their efforts failed, yet again. In 1896

10 Bordin, *Frances Willard,* 160–61. The *Christian Advocate* was the national Methodist newspaper.
11 Bordin, 161–62.
12 Bordin, 165. Remember, laymen had only received the right to be seated at General Conference in 1872, and it was women who would have voted for them at their annual conference sessions.
13 Bordin, 167.

the full General Conference voted to accept women as delegates; consequently, women were first seated as delegates at the 1904 General Conference, after Willard's death.

Nevertheless, she preached. Denied a voice and representation within the institutional church, Willard, along with thousands of other Methodist women, followed her call through her involvement and leadership in reform organizations. Bordin argues that "during the last forty years of the nineteenth century, the Methodist Episcopal Church [MEC] simultaneously constricted and expanded the role of women within the denomination. Women were channeled into a separate [appropriate] sphere—for example, female missionary societies and Sunday school work—but denied the right to preach, to be ordained, or to have a voice in church governing councils."[14] Thus, within the denomination women were given religious authority, but of a specific kind. What unintentionally happened was that the MEC was responsible for the training and advocacy of massive organizations of women who felt empowered by the Holy Spirit and given an unlimited mission field.

Willard's work would extend beyond the institutional church. By 1868, her diary claims more and more attention to the "Woman Question." She was not yet sure of how she would go about addressing the question, but she knew that she would do it through a religious lens. Carolyn DeSwarte analyzed Willard's diaries and concluded, "Her faith would inform both her interpretation of the Woman Question and her response to the issues raised by the most crucial question. She would be a Christian first, and only then a women's rights reformer."[15] Willard was a staunch proponent of the idea that white women's role in this world was to improve the society around them, and she was well versed in how to appeal to white women across the social spectrum. Willard was able to weave together religious and political rhetoric to appeal to all sorts of white women—from those who believed their proper place was in the home to those who believed it was at the ballot box—and convince them all that they had an obligation to improve their world in whatever way they could. Willard excelled at combining "the Enlightenment idealism of the first women's rights advocates with the missionary mentality of rural Protestant women."[16]

And she did so by preaching the Methodist God of love: "The time will come when the human heart will be so much alive that no one could sleep in any given community; if any of that group of human beings were

---

14 Bordin, 167.
15 Gifford, *Writing Out My Heart*, 202.
16 Bordin, *Frances Willard*, 174.

cold, hungry, or miserable."[17] She pushed white women, especially religious women, to "have a new concept of religion."[18] In a similar turn of phrase as John Wesley's, she believed that the core of religion was love, not an internal, self-contained love, but a love that had to be expressed outward, to better the lives of those living among you. She wrote to her beloved Anna Gordon, "The religion of the world is a religion of love; it is a home religion; it is a religion of peace."[19]

As president of the Woman's Christian Temperance Union, Frances Willard was nothing short of a political genius. It was under her leadership that the WCTU grew to be the largest women's organization of her time. Her first institutional campaign was "Home Protection," or what she termed "political housekeeping." While she used the temperance platform of the WCTU, she quickly advocated that the best way to ensure temperance was through white women's suffrage, for why would men, the majority of consumers of hard liquor, ever vote to ban it? Through the vote, white women would, in her words, "make the world home-like" by bringing their moral influence from the home and into the world.[20] By the mid-1880s, the WCTU was an official endorser of white women's suffrage. However, Willard didn't wait until white women had the vote to argue that they could be a powerful influence in society. She used the little power that women already had to argue that they could make a difference in their local communities.

Her boldest and most successful campaign was "Do Everything." In a rapidly changing society, Willard said, "a one-sided movement makes for one-sided advocates." She knew that temperance reform would never be enough to truly make long-lasting change. Instead, the country needed to develop a "corporate" conscience and come to understand that "society" is "a unity which has such relations to every faction thereof that there could be no rest while any lacked food, clothing or shelter or while any were so shackled by the grim circumstances of life that they were unable to develop the best that was in them in body and mind."[21] This is the heart of Wesleyan theology—love acted out. No true Methodist—or person of faith, for that matter—could rest while others suffered. There is a faith-driven moral

17 Bordin, 159.
18 Bordin, 159.
19 Bordin, 159–60.
20 Gifford and Slagell, eds., *Writing Out My Heart: Selections from the Journal of Frances E. Willard, 1855–96* (Chicago: Univ. of Illinois Press, 1995). *Let Something Good Be Said*, 7.
21 Willard, "Minutes of the National Woman's Christian Temperance Union," 1893, 104–5, as quoted in Bordin, *Frances Willard*, 210.

imperative to undo systemic injustice that continuously causes harm and oppresses others.

However, Willard fell short of her Methodist duties by not advocating for universal suffrage. Willard's reforms were largely limited to white women. While the WCTU was open to all, and its "Do Everything" policy offered African American women a chance to advocate for other African Americans through the Department of Colored Work, Willard's own view of African Americans inhibited the WCTU from fully arguing for racial equity alongside gender equity.

In an 1890 interview for the *Voice*, Willard condoned the educational requirements for suffrage, thus limiting suffrage to white women of a certain means only. She believed that illiterate people abused alcohol more frequently than those who were literate, and thus to pass temperance reform, educational requirements were also necessary. Later in the interview, Willard endorsed false beliefs that African American men had to be restrained from raping white women and that this, and only this, was the reason for lynching across the South. This overtly racist stance was not ignored by her contemporaries. Ida B. Wells, a fellow Methodist woman and a journalist, read Willard's words and later republished them in a British newspaper. Wells hoped that showcasing the harm of Willard's words on African American communities and bodies would help garner support for her own anti-lynching campaign. Willard had an opportunity to use the WCTU to begin to dismantle the systemic oppression of African Americans, but instead she gave in to racist sentiment in order to promote white women. This is a stain on her legacy and her work. It is a necessary piece of any conversation that seeks to praise Willard for her political genius, including this one. We can be proud that Willard was Methodist; we can be proud of the work she accomplished for white women; and we can be proud of these things while at the same time critiquing her for racism and the harm it caused.[22]

For Willard, the best way to improve the morality of society was to get more white women involved outside the home. Most historians agree that

> American society embraced with conviction the idea of women's moral superiority, and as women moved into the public sphere, they carried with them that aura of uncorrupted righteousness bestowed on them to justify the importance of their role as guardians of the home and nurturers of children. When the political issue was a moral one, the position

22 "Frances Willard and the 'Race Problem,'" from "Truth-Telling: Frances Willard and Ida B. Wells," Frances Willard House Museum, accessed February 17, 2020, http://scalar.usc.edu/works/willard-and-wells/the-voice-interview.

taken on it by women could not be ignored, especially by men of reform principles who were cloaking their own causes in moral righteousness. The pedestal moved with women into the public sphere and for a brief season elevated their influence in that area.[23]

Willard knew that for white women to eventually desire and advocate for suffrage, she would have to get them used to being in the public sphere. Many white women of her time were of a more conservative mindset and fully believed that a "woman's place was in the home." Willard was one of the most successful women to use the qualities of "true womanhood"—piety, purity, and domesticity—that kept them in the home and convince even the most conservative of women that they could maintain these qualities outside the home. In her WCTU newspaper, the *Union Signal*, she wrote, "What shall we do? Just what we have so long done in home, church and school—be an influence for gentle strength, intelligent patience and wise, heroic counsel. Woman . . . must possess her soul in quietness; she must avoid personalities and push principles to the front."[24] For these women, the rhetoric was the same; their role was the same; it was simply in a new location. Willard gave women a small taste of power but through an avenue that was comfortable, familial, and local.

Who knew the needs of local societies better than its local mothers? Willard argued that they shouldn't listen to national organizations to figure out how to improve their local towns; instead they should look around them, look at the unique needs of their towns, and do everything in their power to improve their local conditions. Willard did not have a singular national agenda for the WCTU. Instead she empowered local factions of the WCTU to figure out their own agendas. This relinquishing of power was nothing short of genius. It gave women a sense of authority, something they did not have outside the home. More important, it allowed many of them, especially the more conservative, to argue that they were maintaining the "proper" roles of a woman because they were using their feminine purity and feminine piety to clean up, even domesticate, their hometowns. In their minds, men had held social power for centuries, and societies were only getting more and more vile. Thus, it was up to the women to step in, use their feminine qualities, and clean up the streets.

This small step of empowering women on the local level was necessary to getting many white women on board with the idea of suffrage. It allowed them to see that they could actually make a difference outside of their

23 Bordin, *Frances Willard*, 188–89.
24 Bordin, 189.

homes. It taught them how to use their voices outside the home for social change. It gave them a small taste of social authority. Willard then would step back in and tell them how suffrage could lead to other reforms—prevention of child labor, safer working conditions for women, temperance laws, access to better health care, and so on. For example, when it came to temperance, Willard argued that since it was mostly men who abused liquor, and mostly women and children who suffered at the hands of these intoxicated men, to both preserve womanhood and protect children, white women had to step in and vote to ban alcohol. They had to have access to the ballot in order to make real change in their own lives and the lives of their children.

During Willard's presidency, the WCTU grew from a small, struggling group focused on the single issue of temperance to the largest women's organization in the country, with a broad program of reform, encompassing temperance, white women's suffrage, women's economic and religious rights, and the support of measures advocated by the rising labor movement. Willard knew that her organizational system was designed to empower women at the local level. The WCTU "became a kind of school to train women for responsible participation in the public life of their country."[25]

Willard was respected by white suffragists and conservative white women alike. After visiting Willard on her deathbed, Susan B. Anthony recalled, "She is dying, and she doesn't know it, and no one around her realizes it. She is lying there, seeing into two worlds, and making more plans than a thousand women could carry out in ten years. Her brain is wonderful. She has the most extraordinary clearness of vision. There should be a stenographer in that room, and every word she utters should be taken down, for every word is golden."[26]

Anna Howard Shaw

Another suffragist, Anna Howard Shaw, knew Frances Willard and was inspired by her. In her memoir, Shaw said of Willard, "I never knew a woman who could grip an audience and carry it with her as she could. She was intensely emotional, and swayed others by emotions rather than by logic."[27]

---

25 Gifford and Slagell, *Let Something Good Be Said,* 7.

26 Gifford and Slagell, "Woman and Temperance (1883)," chap. 9 in *Let Something Good Be Said.*

27 Gifford and Slagell, "Three Articles in the WCTU Newspaper (1881–83)," chap. 7 in *Let Something Good Be Said.*

Like many in her day, Shaw got involved in the women's movement because of the pain she had witnessed in her own mother's life. Shaw was born in England in 1847, but her family quickly moved to the United States, settling in Massachusetts. Looking for financial gain, her father moved her family to what was at the time the frontiers of Michigan. Instead of laboring by his family's side, Shaw's father sought fortune elsewhere, leaving his wife to raise four children on her own, with zero social connections in their new Michigan home. As a result, Shaw's mother had a mental breakdown, suffering under the expectations and isolation of motherhood. Trisha Franzen, a biographer of Shaw, contextualizes this move as Shaw's "first painful step into adulthood and a consciousness that patriarchal power could be dangerous."[28]

Witnessing her mother's pain led Shaw to look for more out of her own life. By age thirteen, Shaw felt a call to preach, but this call was prohibited by her parents, who made her "pledge never to preach" or else forgo an education.[29] Unable to make this pledge, Shaw, at sixteen, sacrificed a formal education and taught school in Michigan to support herself and her family. After years of teaching, she attended a lecture by Rev. Marianna Thompson, a woman who was living the life of which Shaw dreamed. Shaw introduced herself to Reverend Thompson and told her of her own call to ministry. Thompson encouraged Shaw to follow her call but to get an education first. So, at twenty-three, Shaw returned to school at Big Rapids High School. It was here that she was soon discovered by a Methodist woman, Lucy Foot, the school's preceptress. Foot became Shaw's mentor and eventually connected her to a presiding elder of the Methodist Episcopal Church who desired to see women ordained. Dr. H. C. Peck gave Shaw a license to preach, and in 1871 she gave her first official sermon.[30]

For Shaw, preaching in the Methodist Episcopal Church would open many doors that would ultimately lead to a career in women's rights. But for this choice, she faced intense criticism and was even dismissed from her family. Franzen reports that Anna's sister, Mary, ceased all communication

28 Trisha Franzen, *Anna Howard Shaw: The Work of Woman Suffrage* (Chicago: Univ. of Illinois Press, 2014), 25.

29 Anna Howard Shaw, "Select Your Principle of Life," as quoted in Mary D. Pellauer, *Toward a Tradition of Feminist Theology: The Religious Social Thought of Elizabeth Cady Stanton, Susan. B. Anthony, and Anna Howard Shaw* (Brooklyn: Carlson, 1991), 221.

30 Though she was supported by a presiding elder and given pulpits to preach from, her official preaching license was granted two years later, in 1873, by the Big Rapids District Conference of the Methodist Episcopal Church. Franzen, *Anna Howard Shaw,* 39.

with her. Her brother-in-law, George Green, wrote an article for a local news-paper, urging everyone to sever ties with Anna. Her family even tried to bribe her away from the pulpit with an offer of free education if she stopped preaching. However, because she was a licensed preacher, the Methodist Episcopal Church would also support her education, and thus instead of staying with her family, she left for Albion College. Her letters composed dur-ing her studies at Albion showcase Shaw's understanding of her life's calling. Franzen argues that it is here that we first see "the language of an evangelical Methodist" who believed that "God had chosen her path, and she had no choice but to follow."[31] And by 1876, God was leading her to a different type of education. She decided to leave Albion and pursue theological studies at Boston University School of Theology.

Her theological education was a true test of her call. In her own words, "[I]t was an instance of stepping off a solid plank and into space"—a space for which even Shaw's "lively imagination had not prepared [her]." Theo-logical school prepared her not only in terms of exegesis and hermeneutics but also in "what it was to go to bed cold and hungry, to wake up cold and hungry, and to have no knowledge of how long these conditions might con-tinue." Because "women theologians paid heavily for the privilege of being women," she suffered the "physical and mental depression attending mal-nutrition." Her young male classmates "were licensed preachers" and "were given free accommodations in the dormitory" along with a discounted board at a local club. For women "no such kindly provision was made," and Shaw, along with women before and after her, faced a lack of food for the pursuit of graduate theological studies.[32] Methodist theological schools were willing to admit women for theological education, and women were allowed to have a license to preach, but full equality or even decent treatment was never guaranteed. As we'll see in chapter 5, women are still not guaranteed decent treatment or even respect in seminary or in their churches.

While in Albion, Shaw was frequently called upon to preach due to the lack of ministers in the area. And she knew how to use the ministry, for "through it she claimed respectability as well as personal and spiritual inde-pendence." Franzen places Shaw in line with Sojourner Truth as a Methodist woman who used her "religious calling" to "bypass restrictions created by 'mere mortal' men and claim a divine directive to preach."[33] However, in

---

31 Franzen, 41.

32 Anna Howard Shaw, "The Wolf at the Door," chap. 4 in *The Story of a Pioneer*, http://www.gutenberg.org/files/354/354-h/354-h.htm#link2H_4_0009.

33 Franzen, *Anna Howard Shaw*, 7.

Boston, she found the restrictions of men pushed her to malnourishment. Shaw was in competition with "a hundred men, each snatching eagerly at the slightest possibility of employment." When she was asked to preach, she "never knew whether [she] was to be paid for [her] services in cash or in compliments."[34] Shaw pushed herself to the point of starvation, until she was finally discovered and given financial support by the Woman's Foreign Missionary Society. Nevertheless, she preached.

Shaw graduated in 1878 and was given a two-point charge in East Dennis, Massachusetts. When her request for full ordination was refused by the Methodist Episcopal Church, she left and joined the Methodist Protestant Church, which ordained her in 1880. Shaw was placed in a congregation that was "in the hands of two warring factions" of which she was "blissfully ignorant."[35] Unsatisfied with her charges and seeking to do more to help the plight of women, by 1883 Shaw returned to Boston University for a medical degree, even though she "had no intention of practising medicine" but merely meant to "add a certain amount of medical knowledge to [her] mental equipment."[36] Working to save bodies and souls through her studies, she received her MD in 1886. Franzen argues that "she concluded that neither the ministry nor medicine could help [poor women] because those efforts didn't get to the 'foundation of social structure.'"[37] Shaw knew that to get at the root of the systemic injustices that plagued women and children, especially those in living in poverty, she would have to live out her call in a different way.

Her new calling was to the cause of women's equality. After her various degrees, Shaw worked as a lecturer for the Massachusetts Woman Suffrage Association and as head of the Woman's Christian Temperance Union Franchise Department. She left her pulpit ministry, for, in her own words, "deep in my heart, I realized the needs of the outside world." She had heard the words of great women around her—"Mary A. Livermore . . . [,] Julia Ward Howe, Anna Garlin Spencer, Lucy Stone, Mary F. Eastman, and many others"—and she knew that these women were "fighting great battles . . . for suffrage, for temperance, for social purity."[38] While in Boston, Shaw had observed the plight of women firsthand:

---

34 Shaw, "The Wolf at the Door."
35 Shaw, "Shepherd of a Divided Flock," chap. 5 in *Story of a Pioneer.*
36 Shaw, "The Great Cause," chap. 7 in *Story of a Pioneer.*
37 Franzen, *Anna Howard Shaw,* 55.
38 Shaw, "The Great Cause."

Around me I saw women overworked and underpaid, doing men's work
at half men's wages, not because their work was inferior, but because they
were women. Again, too, I studied the obtrusive problems of the poor and
of the women of the streets; and, looking at the whole social situation
from every angle, I could find but one solution for women—the removal
of the stigma of disfranchisement. As man's equal before the law, woman
could demand her rights, asking favors from no one. With all my heart I
joined in the crusade of the men and women who were fighting for her.
My real work had begun.[39]

The best way, reasoned Shaw, to improve the lives of women and the poor
and the most effective way to uplift society in general was by getting women
access to the ballot box. Even though she resigned her pulpit ministry in
1885, Shaw always remained an ordained clergywoman. While her mission field had changed, "she remained a progressive Christian who increasingly valued good works on a large public scale over a particular evangelical
experience of conversion and personal faith."[40] She was now called to the
streets and to the lecture circuit, not the pulpit. It was on the streets and
from the lecture podium that she showcased her concern "with ameliorat-
ing people's lives" instead of "debating theological doctrine or the latest
intellectual development." Franzen argues that "[h]er vibrant and rebellious
Christianity consistently needed to challenge the status quo and established
institutions." For Shaw, "[p]romoting justice was a core part of her religious
duty, and that contributed to her belief that her calling extended far beyond
the walls of her churches."[41]

Shaw was known for her rhetorical skill and her quick wit, and she was
quickly adopted by Susan B. Anthony for full-time suffrage advocacy. What
made Shaw a prominent suffragette was a sermon given to the International
Council of Women in 1888. The National Suffrage Association headed
the council and extended "the invitation to all associations of women in
the trades, professions, and reforms, as well as those advocating political
rights."[42] It was to be an event celebrating the fortieth anniversary of Seneca Falls, the convention that officially organized the white women's campaign for suffrage. Held in Washington, DC, on March 25, 1888, the council
sought to "devise new and more effective methods for securing . . . the

---

39 Shaw.
40 Franzen, *Anna Howard Shaw*, 55.
41 Franzen, 53.
42 Susan B. Anthony and Ida Husted Harper, eds., *The History of Woman Suffrage,
1883–1900* (n.p.: Fowler & Wells, 1902), 4: 125.

equality and justice which [women] have so long and so earnestly sought" in the "State, in the Church, and in the Home."[43] Invitees were not limited to those seeking political reform; the invitation was extended to various organizations: "Literary Clubs, Art Unions, Temperance Unions, Labor Leagues, missionary, Peace, and Moral Purity Societies, Charitable, Professional, Education, and Industrial Associations." The Council was to last eight days, with sixteen public sessions, to "afford ample opportunity for reporting the various phases of woman's work and progress in all parts of the world, during the past forty years."[44]

When the council convened on March 25, 1888, "fifty-three organizations of women, national in character, of a religious, patriotic, charitable, reform, literary, and political nature were represented on the platform by eighty speakers and forty-nine delegates, from England, Ireland, France, Norway, Denmark, Finland, India, Canada, and the United States."[45] The opening day sermon was given by Anna Howard Shaw, "a matchless discourse" entitled "The Heavenly Vision."[46] This sermon is copied verbatim in Susan B. Anthony and Ida Husted Harper's *History of Woman Suffrage*. In the text, Shaw describes David's vision of "a world lost in sin." Men had tried everything in their power to fix the world, but "to no purpose." And there "sat woman, limited by sin, limited by social custom, limited by false theories, limited by bigotry and by creeds," waiting for her chance to remedy the social ills before her.

> At last, in the mute agony of despair, she lifted her eyes above the earth to heaven and away from the jarring strifes which surrounded her, and that which dawned upon her gaze was so full of wonder that her soul burst its prison-house of bondage as she beheld the vision of true womanhood. She knew then it was not the purpose of the Divine that she should crouch beneath the bonds of custom and ignorance. She learned that she was created not from the side of man, but rather by the side of man. The world had suffered because she had not kept her divinely-appointed place.[47]

Here Shaw preached that women had stood by and watched humankind suffer because they had been blinded by false teachings of the church. They

---

43 Anthony and Harper, 125.
44 Anthony and Harper, 126.
45 Anthony and Harper, 127.
46 Anthony and Harper, 128.
47 Shaw, in Anthony and Harper, 128–29.

had been falsely told that they were the reason for sin in the world, and thus they had to sit by and quietly watch the world fall apart around them.

For two millennia, Christians had called on women to be submissive to their husbands based on the view of the punishments of Adam and Eve in Genesis 3. As we now know, this is a perversion of creation. God created man and woman as equals. Bone of bone and flesh of flesh, man and woman were created of the same substance and at the same time. However, churchmen historically interpreted the fall as a result of Eve duping Adam and persuading him to bite the forbitten fruit, so it was her fault that sin entered the world and they were forced from the garden, away from God's grace. Because of Eve's temptation of Adam, God would punish women forevermore with pain in childbirth and compulsory submission to their husbands. Even now when Christians proclaim that women should be submissive, they are calling Christians to celebrate and live into a perverse understanding of creation, instead of calling them to live better lives—lives of equality, which God originally intended us to live. Shaw corrected this error, reminding women that they weren't created to be subservient to men but to be their equal. She then challenged women to rise up, take their proper place beside men, and no longer let the world suffer and inflict suffering because of some false assertion of subservience.

Her message was unifying. She recognized that at the council were gathered women "from the East and the West, the North and the South, women of every land, of every race, of all religious beliefs." They had come together "with one harmonious purpose—that of lifting humanity into a higher, purer, truer life." Of course, they had come to this event with different goals—some sought political equality, some racial equality, some social equality, some temperance reform, and some education reform. However, one thing united them all, and that was that they had come "not to do their own work, but the will of [God] who sent them."[48]

Shaw had given up the pulpit ministry but not her faith or her calling to preach. Since receiving her call in the woods when she was fourteen, she knew that she was on a God-driven mission to make the world around her a better place. This mission led her to be a local pastor in the Methodist Episcopal Church, to seek a theological degree and then a medical degree from Boston University, and to abandon the formal pulpit and instead use her gift of rhetoric to speak to women about their God-given equality to men. Nevertheless, she preached.

---

48 Anthony and Harper, 130–31.

After the International Council of Women, Shaw quickly joined the prominent ranks of suffragists. Susan B. Anthony, or "Aunt Susan" as Shaw called her, knew that the suffrage movement needed to remedy its reputation with religiously minded people. Shaw was her answer. Most people considered Anthony "irreligious" for the sole reason that they would not, according to her, "accept the fact that I am Quaker—or, rather they seem to think a Quaker is an infidel." She made it clear that one of the reasons she needed Shaw was her faith: "I'm glad you are a Methodist, for now they cannot claim that we are not orthodox."[49] Shaw believed that democracy was a divinely created form of government (consistent with her peers at the time). She would frequently connect the voice of the government to the voice of God:

> And you who talk of a great Government in which the voice of God is heard must remember that if "the voice of the people is the voice of God," you will never know what the voice of God in Government is until you get the voice of the people, and the voice of the people has a soprano as well as a bass. You must join the soprano voice of God to the bass voice of God in order to get the harmony of the Divine voice, and then you will have a law which will enable you to say, We are justly ruled.[50]

Well versed in emerging biblical criticism from her time at Boston University School of Theology, Shaw knew that the divine voice spoke with both male and female intonation. Here Shaw poignantly deduced that if a democratic republic is truly the voice of God—as her male peers had so often claimed it was—then it must recognize the various voices of God and not just those that are male. For Susan B. Anthony, Shaw's ordination and religious rhetoric gave the suffrage campaign a new sense of religious authority, with Shaw, at least in Aunt Susan's mind, exemplifying "orthodox of the orthodox."[51]

Some historians identify religion as the reason women remained in the home, and this was true for some women. But for many Methodist women, their faith was the very thing that propelled them from their homes and into the public sphere; and in fact, "a number of suffrage leaders were pioneering women ministers."[52] Shaw was exceptional among other Methodist women since she had received a seminary education and was ordained. She knew how to deconstruct the religiously based arguments that had been oft stated by men and women to limit women to the confines of the

---

49 Shaw, "Aunt Susan," chap. 9 in *Story of a Pioneer.*
50 Pellauer, *Toward a Tradition of Feminist Theology,* 231.
51 Shaw, "Aunt Susan."
52 Franzen, *Anna Howard Shaw,* 7.

home. Conversant in religious language, hermeneutics, and domestic rhetoric, Shaw knew how to connect with women around her, both progressive and conservative, religious and non. She claimed, "Every suffragist I have ever met has been a lover of home; and only the conviction that she is fighting for her home, her children, for other women, or for all of these, has sustained her in her public work."[53]

Shaw used her quick wit and her religious authority as an ordained clergywoman to rise to the ranks of president of the National American Woman Suffrage Association (NAWSA) in 1904, a post she would serve until 1916. Under her leadership the association grew from seventeen thousand members to more than two hundred thousand, and the annual budget increased fourfold.[54] The number of states with enfranchised women increased from four in 1906 to twelve by 1914.[55] According to Franzen, under Shaw's leadership the NAWSA evolved from "a struggling voluntary association directed by a small group of otherwise 'white, middle-class and native-born' women to a professional organization headquartered in New York City with salaried executive workers and a sophisticated publicity department." Under her leadership the organization also began to reach beyond white, middle-class women, to include "working women, college students, men, and many politicians," efforts at which Willard substantially failed.[56]

For many of the suffragettes, however, Shaw went against social standards of womanhood in too many ways. She was outspoken, witty, and quick to debate, "a character who had learned early that following the rules didn't get you very far if you were poor and a girl."[57] Women's historians have long ignored Shaw's work and her contribution to women's history. Franzen says that Shaw was overlooked for many reasons, one because she was an immigrant from a poor community, which made her, in Shaw's own words, "less like a lady than anything else in the world."[58] This self-description can have many interpretations. Shaw knew from the time she was a child that she was unlike other girls. She "had created an unusual identity for herself," argues Franzen, as she preferred to be "out in the public rather than by her mother's side within the home." It was in the public realm that she felt most comfortable, and it was her engagement with the public realm from an early age that

53 Shaw, "Building a Home," chap. 12 in *Story of a Pioneer*.
54 Shaw, "Vale!," chap. 17 in *Story of a Pioneer*.
55 Shaw, "The Passing of Aunt Susan," chap. 10 in *Story of a Pioneer*.
56 Franzen, *Anna Howard Shaw*, 2.
57 Franzen, 3.
58 Franzen, 5.

"demonstrate[ed] her preference for nontraditional activities."[59] According to Franzen, Shaw was "gender-variant in both her personal and professional characteristics and preferences." In other words, "she lived, partnered [with], and supported a family all outside of what we now term heteropatriarchy."[60] Shaw surrounded herself with powerful women, like Susan B. Anthony and Frances Willard. Her partner for more than thirty years was Anthony's niece, Lucy E. Anthony, her "beloved."[61] Shaw pushed the boundaries of woman-hood by pushing the boundaries of family. She constructed a chosen family, "one neither constrained nor endorsed by the state."[62]

Shaw and Willard

In this vein, Shaw and Frances Willard were similar. Willard, also, redefined the home and the family at a time when the home/family was an expected center of society. Also a lifelong single woman, Willard broke off a couple of engagements to men but lived her entire life surrounded by women. Her longest partner and lifelong companion was Anna Gordon, who remained by Willard's side as her devoted secretary. Willard was a champion of rede-fining women's roles in the home as equals to their husbands through a reexamination of biblical commands for obedience and subservience. And she expanded the notion of family beyond the nuclear family.

Willard's Methodist faith had taught her that family exists beyond biol-ogy, and she used the Methodist lingo of referring to her colleagues and friends as "brothers and sisters." This was not only a reference to her faith but also a way of equalizing the status between her and her male comrades. However, using the rhetoric of these men, it also elevated the status of women through the stereotypical ideology of true womanhood. If women were the moral center of the home and if the home were expanded beyond the confines of the household to encompass the brothers and sisters of society at large, then women were now the moral superiors of all humanity. According to Willard, "'home' was not so much a place as an attitude: one of welcome, care, respectfulness, and affection." Thus, for Willard, home protection did not encourage women of the WCTU to stay in their houses and protect their nuclear families. Home protection was "her call to 'make the world homelike,'" but it "cannot be reduced to mere sloganizing." Willard

---

59 Franzen, 21.
60 Franzen, 6.
61 Franzen, 64–65, 75–76.
62 Franzen, 76.

intended that home protection "be understood as the heading for her broadest reform agenda and her hope for a world transfigured."[63] Home protection encouraged women to step outside of their homes, stake a claim in the social strata, and demand that their moral voices be heard.

Going against familial norms places Shaw and Willard in a long line of Methodists. Before Methodism became "mainline," it was considered an "enthusiastic" religion. When you joined a Methodist society, you went against cultural norms. Many early Methodists pushed the boundaries of social norms by mixing genders, classes, and races, and proclaiming that all who came before God and accepted God's grace were equal and worthy of love. Its equalizing gospel message went against an American culture that enslaved people according to race and limited their full involvement in society based on class (e.g., property owners) and gender. Joining a Methodist society often resulted in people being expelled by their families. Thus, early Methodist language discussed the chosen family, the church family, the Christian family.[64] In other words, it is a very Methodist thing to forgo nuclear families and choose families based on a common bond. Shaw and Willard did this, continuing the Methodist tradition of being countercultural but doing so with a feminist, some might say even queer, flair.

Neither Frances Willard nor Rev. Anna Howard Shaw lived to see the passage of white women's suffrage by Congress in 1919 and ratification by the states in 1920. Neither lived to see women receive full membership and ordinations rights within the main branch of the Methodist movement in 1956. Picking up where these women left off were other great Methodist women, including Georgia Harkness. In her book *Women in Church and Society*, Harkness situates the women's movement in the midst of the other revolutions of post–World War II America, including civil rights and anti-Vietnam protests.

In post–World War II society, women gained more rights both within society at large and within the Methodist Church, and they did so using very similar arguments to those of Willard and Shaw. In 1952, the General Conference of the Methodist Church convened and, yet again, denied the rights of full conference membership and ordination to women. In Harkness's words, this matter "was passed over rapidly with the usual rejection, to the accompaniment of considerable laughter."[65] Not only was it implausible that women

---

63 Gifford, *Writing Out My Heart,* 17–18.
64 See Christine Leigh Heyrman, *Southern Cross: The Beginnings of the Bible Belt* (Chapel Hill: Univ. of North Carolina Press, 1998).
65 Georgia Harkness, *Women in Church and Society* (Nashville: Abingdon, 1972), 30.

be granted full clerical rights to ordination; it was thought to be a laughing matter that they kept trying to gain them. These women were scorned and held up as objects of ridicule. Largely since the formation of the Methodist Episcopal Church in 1784, women had argued for their right to preach, for the right for their voices to be heard. They were granted local preachers licenses by the mid-nineteenth century, allowing such women as Anna Howard Shaw to preach locally within the Methodist Episcopal Church, but they were not granted full membership in the conference or through ordination. Thus, they did not have representation or a voice at General Conference.

After 1952, "the women present resolved that it was no longer to be treated as a laughing matter!" In the midst of the burgeoning women's movement, Methodist women made a stand within their denomination first. The "Woman's Division of Christian Service" sent in "over 2,000 petitions on the subject" of women's ordination "to the General Conference of 1956." Harkness recalls sitting "in silence," knowing that if she chose to participate in the men's debate, it would only hurt the women's cause, for women's silence, to that point, was "the surest way to get something passed." After "three [or] four hours of vigorous debate on the floor of the Conference, mainly between men on both sides of the issue," there was a vote in favor of "the full eradication of official sex discrimination in the ministry of The Methodist Church."[66]

It is easy to argue that without the efforts of these women and the men who supported them, their speeches, their sermons, their leadership—within the WCTU, NAWSA, and the Methodist tradition—and their faith, suffrage would not have been granted for white women in 1920 nor ordination in 1956. Under Shaw's and Willard's leadership, the Woman's Christian Temperance Union and the National American Woman's Suffrage Association became the largest and most respected women's organizations of their time. We can see their influence in women such as Georgia Harkness. They reminded thousands of white women of their dignity and equality before the law and before God. They used their faith as a propeller to launch their own careers in the public and political realms and used a faith-centered rhetoric to connect to white women who thought they weren't worthy or made for the vote, the pulpit, or full equality. They embraced John Wesley's theology of love as a lived-out, disciplined, and practical notion of the divine. They embodied social holiness through social justice. They strove to ensure that through their own lifetimes, and hopefully beyond, social and systemic injustice would be thwarted. These two women are rarely considered together

---

66 Harkness, 30.

and seldom considered as beacons of the women's suffrage movements. Their frequent use of religious rhetoric, their willingness to challenge the notion of family life, their choosing of lifelong female partners over traditional marriage, and their sharp wit have prevented their full inclusion in the story of suffrage. But they are worthy of inclusion for their sheer astuteness, for their commitment to be who they were, for refusing to conform to social standards so that they might dismantle those standards, and for their persistence in preaching, *no matter what.*

Discussion Questions

1. What women in your own life inspired you to vote or engage politically?
2. What women in your own life inspired you to engage in ministry or follow a call to ministry?
3. What obstacles have you faced when you have sought to exercise a political, public, or religious voice? Why do you think these obstacles exist?
4. What will you take away from the lives and ministries of Frances E. Willard and Anna Howard Shaw?
5. What are the limitations on voting rights in your state?
6. How will you ensure that *all* people have the right to vote?

TWO: RACIAL EQUITY

> And where were the Methodist women in the civil rights movement? Many were marching. Others were serving coffee to marchers. Some were writing letters to Senators and Representatives. Hundreds of Methodist women were working to prevent violence in the schools of their communities. Other tried to uproot segregation in churches and communities. They were voting for upstanding public officials and joining groups concerned with drafting just state and city laws. Many, yes, many, many thousands of Methodist women, white and black, were engaged in differing ways in the civil rights movement.
>
> —Thelma Stevens, *Legacy for the Future*

Methodism has multiple reputations in America. Some view it as one of the more progressive denominations; others see it as yet another institution that continuously oppresses minority groups. When it comes to racial equality, Methodism is both.

John Wesley and other Methodists fought against slavery. Early Methodist ministers who enslaved people had their licenses revoked. However, after Wesley's death, Methodism in America tried to gain power in society, which associated power with whiteness, and enslaved people on a massive scale. Thus, Methodism compromised and allowed Methodists, even preachers and bishops, to own slaves. However, some Methodists could not understand how a Christian denomination that proclaimed to follow the liberationist message of Jesus could justify enslaving others. This impasse caused a schism in 1844, when the Methodist Episcopal Church divided into a northern and a southern branch. These branches reunited in 1939, but did so again only with a compromise on race: all African American members, clergy, and bishops were institutionally segregated into the Central Jurisdiction. While the Central Jurisdiction was officially ended in 1968 with the merger that created The United Methodist Church, United Methodism has never fully acknowledged its racist past nor how this racist past infiltrates parts of the denomination today.

This chapter exposes some of the systemic racism that was ingrained in earlier Methodist denominations and shows how Methodist women through the Woman's Division sought to undo that racism at its core through education, legislation, and protest. Like the Methodist women who fought for suffrage and for women's equality, Methodist women were at the fore-front of conversations about race at a time when society understood racial difference and inequality as status quo. It was their Methodist faith that propelled these women forward, believing truly that in God's eyes there is no slave or free person, for we are all equal and all deserving of equitable lives. Despite intense internal and external opposition, nevertheless, they preached racial equity.

Thelma Stevens

Thelma Stevens was a Southern Methodist woman who "had both great love for her church and disappointment with some of its policies."[1] Born in 1902 in Mississippi, she witnessed firsthand the racism of the South primarily through its educational segregation. After graduating high school, Stevens found herself, not of her own accord, witnessing the lynching of a black man, an incident that she called "the most devastating experience of my life." From that moment on she dedicated her life to "working for the basic fairness and justice and safety for black people."[2] She initially avoided ministry because the church "was too bigoted," but in her graduate studies she learned of a different way to do church, a new way to preach. At a Methodist institution, Scarritt College for Christian Workers in Nashville, Tennessee, Stevens discovered "an academic climate influenced by the social gospel

---

1   Ellen Blue, *Women United for Change: 150 Years in Mission* (New York: United Methodist Women, 2019), 99.
2   Stevens, as quoted in Blue, 99.

and by forward-thinking southerners whose social consciousness led them to rub against the map of the southern social fabric," specifically through "a concern and passion for helping to root out racism."[3] Her Methodist education would lead her to combat racial injustice within the Methodist Church. The bulk of historical information found in this chapter comes from Thelma Stevens's own witness as recorded in her published history of the Woman's Division's work between 1948 and 1968, *Legacy for the Future*.[4]

Theresa Hoover

Another Methodist woman who will figure prominently in this chapter is Theresa Hoover, who "'spent her entire professional life in the women's mission organizations of The United Methodist Church' and its predecessor, the Methodist Church."[5] In 1971, looking back on her life and ministry, Hoover wrote, "Much of the missionary movement began because women discovered themselves and their potential and no longer were content to sit at home under a shade tree waiting for husbands to bring home news of the world."[6] Hoover was moved to do more. After graduating from Philander Smith College in Little Rock, Arkansas, she began to work at the Little Rock Methodist Council. Through this work she was elected to the Woman's Division, where she served as a field worker. By 1968, her continued witness and the Woman's Division devotion to racial equity led to her holding "the highest staff position ever occupied by a black woman in The United Methodist Church or its predecessor churches" as the chief executive of the Woman's Division of the General Board of Global Ministries.[7]

Methodist History

In 1844 the Methodist Episcopal Church, the first official denomination of Methodism within the United States, split into a northern and a southern church over the morality of slavery. The Methodist Episcopal Church, South, continued to allow its bishops, ministers, and members to enslave people,

---

3 Stevens, in Blue, 99.
4 Thelma Stevens, *Legacy for the Future: The History of Christian Social Relations in the Woman's Division of Christian Service, 1940–1968* (Cincinnati: Women's Division, Board of Global Ministries, United Methodist Church, 1978).
5 Blue, *Women United for Change*, 101.
6 As quoted in Blue, 101.
7 Blue, 102. The Women's Division was the successor organization to the Woman's Division of the Methodist Church.

while the northern Methodist Episcopal Church continued to disavow enslavement, establishing it as a bar to ministry and membership. Many of the current divisions within Methodism have their root in this initial split. The question of slavery was one of the first to bring to light a difference in biblical interpretation. Northern Methodists emphasized the biblical message of doing good, loving God, and loving neighbor as the most important and consistent message throughout the Bible, an emphasis that would continue throughout the twentieth century as society changed and challenged traditional interpretations of scripture. For example, it was within northern Methodism that Boston personalism, a theological position that prioritizes human action to better the world around us and thus an apt theology for Methodists who uphold Wesley's notion of practical divinity, first began to gain traction and heavily influence Methodist theology in the twentieth century.[8] Southern Methodists relied on the Bible verses that emphasized docility of slaves and obedience to masters to justify their racist and abhorrent stances. After the Civil War, in the days of the Jim Crow South, Southern Methodists were known members of the reemerging Ku Klux Klan. It was also well known that some Methodists participated in lynching black men. It is undeniable that Methodism has a racist past, and it is only through learning, acknowledging, and apologizing for this racist past that we can even begin to move forward toward racial reconciliation.

Perhaps the most egregious movement in twentieth-century Methodist history and one that would define the work of the Woman's Division for the duration of the existence of the Methodist Church, was the creation of the Central Jurisdiction in 1939, which condoned and religiously sanctioned institutional racism. Almost one hundred years after the division that split the Methodist Episcopal Church into north and south, the two denominations came back together, along with the Methodist Protestant Church.[9] The three Methodist traditions merged to form the Methodist Church, which would exist until 1968. Talks to begin the reunification of the northern and southern branches had begun decades earlier, but there had never been an agreed-upon way to secure racial equality. The northern branch, the Methodist Episcopal Church, had drawn all-black annual conferences that held most of their black ministers and members. The Methodist Episcopal

---

8   Andrew Langford, *Practical Divinity: Theology in the Wesleyan Tradition*, 2nd ed. (Nashville: Abingdon Press, 1995).

9   Recall from chapter 1 that the Methodist Protestant Church was the denomination responsible for ordaining Anna Howard Shaw. They had been ordaining women since, but in this 1939 merger they would cease.

Church, South, was not fond of this because, in their eyes, it gave too much authority to black ministers. The southern branch preferred their own model of giving black Methodists an entirely different denomination, as they had after the Civil War, when all black members and ministers of the Methodist Episcopal Church, South, were sectioned off into the Colored Methodist Episcopal Church.[10] The agreed-upon compromise was the creation of a Central Jurisdiction. Larger than an annual conference and not as disconnected as a separate denomination, the Central Jurisdiction was institutionalized racism. The Methodist churches in the United States were divided into five regionally based white jurisdictions (which still exist today) and one racially based jurisdiction, the Central Jurisdiction. All black members, ministers, and bishops were placed in the Central Jurisdiction. From its inception, it was abhorrent and controversial. One of the main groups to combat the formation and existence of the Central Jurisdiction was the Woman's Division of Christian Service and Local Church Activities of the Board of Missions.[11]

The Woman's Division

The Woman's Division was the primary agency through which Methodist women sought to enact public, social, and political change both within the denomination itself and in society at large. Formed in the 1939 merger, the 1940 *Discipline* mandated the Woman's Division to "seek to make real and effective the teachings of Jesus as applied to individual, class, racial and national relationships." It continued, "It shall endeavor to enlist the participation of church women in such questions as have a moral and religious significance or an important bearing on public welfare."[12] The new Woman's Division was the result of six different women's organizations from three different denominations coming together to "unify women of varied commitments" whose members "became 'one in spirit with many gifts.'"[13] A compromise that is often overlooked in the 1939 merger involves women

---

10 The Colored Methodist Episcopal Church has since changed its name to the Christian Methodist Episcopal Church and is still in existence today.

11 Hereafter referred to simply as the Woman's Division.

12 Stevens, *Legacy for the Future*, 21.

13 Previous organizations that merged together to form the Woman's Division were the Women's Home Missionary Society (MEC), the Woman's Foreign Missionary Society (MEC), the Wesleyan Service Guild (MEC), the Ladies' Aid Society (MEC), the Women's Missionary Council (MECS), and the Woman's Convention (MPC). See Stevens, 11–13, 16.

specifically. If you remember from chapter 1, the Methodist Protestant church ordained women—including Rev. Anna Howard Shaw. However, the MEC and MEC South did not and would not. Thus, in this 1939 merger, one of the only Methodist traditions that ordained women ceased to ordain women. Methodist women would have to wait until 1956 to be recognized again as worthy of ordination as full members of the annual conference. Thus, the Woman's Division became a central component for women who wanted to maintain some sort of religious authority after their ordination was stripped from them. For those who had a call to ministry, a call to preach, they found an avenue to express this call in and through the Woman's Division. Nevertheless, they preached.

From the creation of the Methodist Church, the Woman's Division recognized the Central Jurisdiction as "such [a] compromise that no Christian church with integrity could long survive in spirit without an overhaul." It was a compromise of the most "degrading kind" that was "rationalized as being a means to safeguard union and build unity." But it did just the opposite for the women of the Woman's Division. They critiqued the beginning of the new denomination for condoning "segregation 'structured in' for the whole world to see." The Woman's Division knew that "there were other crises too, but none so visible and devastating in the eyes of the world's millions of oppressed people of color."[14] From its beginning, the Woman's Division was a rallying cry for action against social injustice, even within the boundaries of its own church. They cried, "We cannot retire into sanctuaries and enjoy our religion!"[15] Its stated goal was "to help women understand and apply the Christian Gospel to collective and personal life . . . through better understanding of the value which Jesus Christ himself placed upon the individual and through personal and collective effort to change social conditions."[16] It continued, "There is a clarion call to Christians in the U.S. to combat all forms of intolerance against minorities, whether in stable local communities, in new national defense projects, in settlement of refugees, citizenship for aliens, or other areas that concern the life of minorities."[17]

This early concern for minorities would frame the work of most of the Woman's Division. One of the foremost goals of the Woman's Division was

---

14 Stevens, 17.
15 From the third official letter of the Woman's Division to its members, written October 15, 1940. Stevens, 20.
16 Stevens, 22.
17 Stevens, 26.

to unite women across regional, racial, and denominational difference. They wanted "to find ways to *unite* Methodist women across the nation. They were segmented by their historical roots in three different denominations; by their structures, which included five regional jurisdictions and the one segregated racial jurisdiction; and by their division into more than a hundred annual conferences."[18]

The Woman's Division did not just put out pithy statements about racial equity; they actively lived out their theology of racial equity. In 1942, at the First Assembly of the Board of Missions, their parent agency, held in St. Louis, the hotel where they were scheduled to convene would not host black people. Before the meeting, the Woman's Division submitted a recommendation to the executive committee, asking the Board of Missions to find a different location for the meeting. Their letter stated, "The department feels that the executive committee of the Board of Missions should restudy the matter, under advisement, and if necessary seek another place for the meeting where segregation of membership will not be necessary." It also requested that all future planning only consider places where segregation would not be necessary in order to uphold "the Christian ideals of democracy." The basis of their argument was that "the church had no right to subject any member to second class citizenship or relegate anyone to less than free and equal accommodations." The Woman's Division was ultimately successful, and the assembly was moved to Columbus, Ohio, where one hotel was fully inclusive of all humanity.[19]

One of the Woman's Division larger events was the National Seminar. This semiannual event consisted of for-college-credit or audited courses held at various Methodist seminaries. The National Seminar was held at seminaries such as Garrett Bible Seminary in Evanston, Illinois, or Iliff School of Theology in Denver, Colorado, which did not enforce segregationist policies. In 1947, the National Seminar wrote three recommendations for the Woman's Division to take to the 1948 General Conference. The first two dealt directly with the authority of the General Conference, with the first focused on the social and spiritual needs of American families and the second for the extension of full clergy rights to women. The third recommendation was directed to the Woman's Division itself, as it called the organization to "lead . . . in race relations by recruiting, training, and the employment of more colored personal [sic] in its staff, and for service in its institutions at

---

18 Stevens, 35.
19 Stevens, 35–36.

home and abroad . . . Further that the offices of the division should include members of minority races."[20]

The same National Seminar also created a Special Committee on Racial Practices, whose first report was released in 1949 and included a thoroughly researched and well-written book, Pauli Murray's *States' Laws on Race and Color.* This book "survey[ed] . . . racial practices of institutions related to the [Woman's] [D]ivision and on laws governing racial policies in foreign lands where the [Woman's] [D]ivision had work."[21] As the first book to compile data on racial policies both within the United States and internationally, it became a profound resource for civil rights attorneys (including Thurgood Marshall).[22] It was published broadly in 1951 by request of the Woman's Division. It showed "the great scope of discrimination within the land." Its researcher and author, "Miss Murray[,] awakened many Christian women to the job ahead in changing unjust laws and made a vital contribution to the civil rights movement in the next decade." The Woman's Division ensured that the book was placed in "600 college and university libraries and in many public libraries" as well as "given [to] the Methodist agencies and institutions." The importance of this work cannot be overstated, for "the survey made it plain that segregation was practiced even where no laws required it." Thus, the Woman's Division was at the forefront of exposing that, even outside of the Jim Crow South, racism and segregation were the unofficial law of the land. The Woman's Division made its mission the dissolution of racial structures and the lifting up of minority voices.[23]

From the information gathered, it was recommended that the Woman's Division "authorize the formulation of a 'Charter on Racial Policies and Practices of the Woman's Division' to be submitted to the Division at the next annual meeting."[24] This policy began with the affirming statement "1. We believe that God is the Father of all people of all races and we are [God's] children in one family." It continued to affirm that "the personality of every human being is sacred" and that everyone has a "right" to "opportunities for fellowship and service, for personal growth, and for freedom in every aspect of life." It called the "visible church of Jesus Christ" to "demonstrate these principles within its own organization and program." It more specifically called the Woman's Division to "build in every area it may touch, a

20 Stevens, 41–42.

21 Blue, *Women United for Change,* 84.

22 Blue, 84.

23 See also Alice Knotts, *Fellowship of Love: Methodist Women Changing American Racial Attitudes, 1920–1968* (Nashville: Kingswood Books, 1996), 195–97.

24 Stevens, *Legacy for the Future,* 50.

fellowship and social order without racial barriers." Finally, "progress" would only be met if the "policies on which the Woman's Division is determined to move in order to come nearer the ideal" were emphatically declared.[25]

The charter then continued beyond belief statements to lay out the exact policies of how those beliefs were to become reality. First, staff at the Woman's Division would be "selected on the basis of qualifications without regard for race." The division sought to "employ all missionaries, deaconesses, and other workers, regardless of racial or national background" as long as they showed "effective work in the field to which they will be sent." It opened all of the Woman's Division's "facilities and opportunities offered" by the organization "to all people without discrimination because of racial or national background." The charter called on local boards to combat local laws and customs that condoned racism and segregation by "creating a public opinion which may result in changing such laws and customs." The Woman's Division was self-aware, asking that all of its "promotional plans . . . take into account the various racial groups within its organizational pattern." It tasked its auxiliary societies with "guidance toward the integration of all groups into the life and work of the church." The charter then directly called out the existence of the Central Jurisdiction and urged that all "Summer schools sponsored by the Board of Missions," "Workshops, seminars, and institutes," "Local Societies and Guilds," and "All Jurisdiction and Conference Societies" seek a "working relationship across racial" and jurisdictional lines. This Charter of Racial Policies was expected to be ratified by each jurisdiction and conference in order to be implemented in an organized and effective manner.[26] It focused on racial justice and equity within the Woman's Division and its auxiliary organizations, seeking to undermine institutional segregation via the Central Jurisdiction by providing black Methodists with equal access to denominational organizations and programming.[27]

However, within one decade, the Woman's Division would realize that this original charter, while bold, was not bold enough. It only sought to eradicate racism within the Woman's Division. So, in 1962, they drafted a Second Charter of Racial Policies, which sought an "enlarged vision": "Eliminate all segregated structures and practices within [the Methodist Church]; Build fellowship and membership in local churches without regard to race; Achieve racial justice in the whole of U.S. society; and Support and strengthen worldwide movements for basic human rights and fundamental freedoms of all

25 Stevens, 64.
26 Stevens, 64–65.
27 See also Knotts, *Fellowship of Love*, 197–99.

peoples."[28] Moving beyond their own organization, the Second Charter of Racial Policies aimed to eradicate racism and segregation within the entire denomination and in the United States. A third charter was written in 1978 and adopted by the entire United Methodist Church as a means to confront and dismantle racism through education around "affirmative action and white privilege."[29]

At its 1954 assembly, the Woman's Division officially adopted the first Charter for Racial Policies. During its meeting, the Supreme Court ruled in *Brown v. the Board of Education*, finding the segregationist policies of the American education system to be unconstitutional. The Woman's Division was the first agency of the Methodist Church to respond to the ruling. It stated:

> We rejoice that the highest tribunal of justice in this land, the Supreme
> Court of the United States, proclaimed on May 17, 1954 that segregation
> in public education anywhere in this nation is an infringement of the
> Constitution and a violation of the Fourteenth Amendment. We accept
> our full Christian responsibility to work through church and community
> channels to speed the process of transition from segregated schools to a
> new pattern of justice and freedom.[30]

Per their mission, the Woman's Division didn't just release this comment. Through the leadership of Mrs. Dorothy Tilly of Atlanta, Georgia, the Woman's Division combined their newly written Charter of Racial Policies with the Supreme Court decision "as springboards to get women moving to implement both."[31] By the fall of 1954 until 1968, Mrs. Tilly "called together 200 southern women—black and white, Protestant, Catholic, and Jew—to convene" each year "in Atlanta as The Fellowship of the Concerned." Through this collaboration "they developed plans and strategies directed toward *two primary goals*: justice in the courts for the poor and the Blacks and implementation of the Supreme Court mandate for desegregation of schools."[32] As the collaboration proved successful, women from "New Orleans and Little Rock, from Jackson, Mississippi and Birmingham," came to Atlanta to learn their strategies.

Working to support desegregation efforts, members of the Woman's Division "founded, joined, or lobbied existing Human Relations Councils in

---

28 Stevens, *Legacy for the Future*, 90.
29 Blue, *Women United for Change*, 84.
30 Stevens, *Legacy for the Future*, 69.
31 Knotts, *Fellowship of Love*, 200–202.
32 Stevens, *Legacy for the Future*, 70, emphasis original.

numerous locations, including Greensboro and Nashville." Before *Brown v. the Board of Education*, the organization had tried desegregating some of its own schools quietly so as to avoid public criticism. After the ruling, it announced that Methodist women were finally fully allowed to "expand our program of racial integration in these institutions and expect our schools to stand by, ready to enroll students and to appoint faculty regardless of race or color."[33] In 1952, Scarritt College for Christian Workers in Nashville, Tennessee, was integrated. But "the Methodist Church lagged behind the Woman's Division in integrating its institutional ministries." Seeking to correct this, the Woman's Division petitioned the 1956 General Conference to study their own institutions. They asked "that the institutions of the church, local churches, colleges, universities, theological schools, hospitals, and home carefully study their policies and practices as they relate to race, making certain that these policies and practices are Christian."[34] Using language that equated desegregation with Christian practices, the Woman's Division challenged any institutional effort to keep segregation within its denominational ranks. In their eyes, anything that prioritized one group of humanity over another was unchristian.

Women of the Woman's Division supported civil rights not only through internal policies and the desegregation of schools. They directly supported the civil rights movement, propelled forward through the voice of Rev. Dr. Martin Luther King Jr. As Thelma Stevens wrote:

> And where were the Methodist women in the civil rights movement? Many were marching. Others were serving coffee to marchers. Some were writing letters to Senators and Representatives. Hundreds of Methodist women were working to prevent violence in the schools of their communities. Other tried to uproot segregation in churches and communities. They were voting for upstanding public officials and joining groups concerned with drafting just state and city laws. Many, yes, many, many thousands of Methodist women, white and black, were engaged in differing ways in the civil rights movement.[35]

Methodist women were everywhere, doing anything and everything they could to combat racism. In every avenue, they preached. They preached using their bodies, their voices, and their witness. The Woman's Division, like the Woman's Christian Temperance Union, recognized that women

---

33 Woman's Division *Journal* as quoted in Knotts, *Fellowship of Love*, 202.
34 Knotts, 203.
35 Stevens, *Legacy for the Future,* 94.

were all different and would have different levels of comfort when it came to political involvement, especially when it came to as controversial an issue as racial equality in the 1960s. Some felt comfortable marching, being in the public eye. Others felt more comfortable supporting those who marched, sitting on the sidelines, cheering them on. And others felt uncomfortable being in the public eye but still used their voices via their pens to write their representatives about the horrors of racism. Nevertheless, they preached.

In the early 1960s, Rev. Dr. King advocated nonviolent action. In 1960, four African American students at North Carolina Agricultural and Technical College staged a sit-in at Woolworth's lunch counter in Greensboro. After being repeatedly denied service, they decided to physically make a statement that they deserved to be treated equally. Unlike the bus boycotts, which required absence, historian Alice Knotts rightly reminds us that sit-ins required nonviolent bodily presence. Thus, participating in a sit-in increased the odds of bodily harm, harassment, arrest, and even death.[36] The Greensboro sit-in led to other sit-ins across the nation. In 1960, students of twenty-seven colleges and universities in eleven different states participated in sit-ins.

Since there was an increased danger for those participating in sit-ins, the Woman's Division adopted a statement supporting the rights of students to engage in this nonviolent form of protest:

> The Woman's Division endorses the method of nonviolence which many students are practicing in the sit-in demonstrations. We believe these demonstrations offer to all Christians in this disturbed hour an opportunity for Christian witness. We urge Methodist women everywhere to study the facts which will enable them to understand, interpret, and undergird these students. We believe that every local church should seek in the context of the Gospel to clarify its position on the race issue.[37]

This statement is not only supportive, but it also explicitly calls sit-ins an opportunity for a Christian to engage in witness. It called Methodist women to educate themselves on the matters at hand before making judgments about what students were doing. And it used the voice of the gospel to justify the students' right to protest racial injustice. The statement continued and called out law enforcement for making "unfair and discriminatory arrests of student leaders," and it demanded "equal protection under

---

36 Knotts, *Fellowship of Love,* 219.
37 Stevens, *Legacy for the Future,* 95.

the law." To put the statement in a bit more context, Vanderbilt University School of Divinity, a Methodist seminary in Nashville, Tennessee, had recently expelled a student, James Lawson, a minister and former missionary, from the Divinity School for organizing and participating in a local sit-in demonstration. His expulsion was a common occurrence, as universities sought to undermine the rights of students to participate in the civil rights movement, especially across the South, in order to not offend their often white donors. Lawson participated in a local sit-in, was arrested, and was expelled by the Divinity School.

However, the faculty of the Divinity School wrote a public letter, signed by fourteen of its sixteen faculty, declaring that they did not support Lawson's expulsion. The Woman's Division joined the faculty and urged Lawson's immediate reinstatement, "expressing profound regret over the expulsion."[38] It then asked other Methodist women to do the same for other students. Women could support these sit-ins by "call[ing] your local law enforcement" to ensure "that the rights of the students to protest are protected"; by "offer[ing] patronage and public support of . . . restaurants when they extend the service of their facilities to non-white patrons"; and "urging the repeal of any local ordinances that violate human rights."[39] Once again, the Woman's Division offered varying levels of political engagement to more women. From calling local law enforcement to dining somewhere that opened their doors and tables to all people, there were multiple avenues to being a social justice advocate.

Stevens reminds us, however, that not all Methodist women supported the civil rights movement. Just as some Methodist women supported slavery and some did not believe that women deserved the right to vote, some Methodist women "sided with those to block change" to civil rights reform. However, those directly involved with the Woman's Division "supported the movement in every way it could" through workshops, seminars, education, and presence.[40]

From anti-lynching, to desegregation, to sit-ins, Methodist women preached at the forefront of the civil rights movement, and they didn't stop there. By the late 1950s, voting rights was one of the predominant issues of the civil rights movement. The Woman's Division began hosting Citizenship Brunches to help Methodist women educate themselves on ballot issues, including access to the ballot. This program was "designed to

---

38 Knotts, *Fellowship of Love,* 221.
39 Stevens, *Legacy for the Future,* 96–97.
40 Stevens, 94.

cultivate churchwomen as citizens more active in local politics."[41] Brunches focused on the political platforms of local candidates and local issues. Here, women learned how and where to register to vote; learned what prevented people, mostly African Americans, from having access to the ballot; and learned how they could help expand voting rights to ensure that all people have access to the ballot. After having read "The Christian and Responsible Citizenship," members of the Woman's Division largely supported legislation that prosecuted those who prohibited or limited access to voter registration or the ballot box. Methodist women were called on to help literally open the doors so that African American men and women could register to vote, submit their votes, and ensure that their votes were accurately counted. For two decades, Methodist women and leaders within the Woman's Division worked to ensure equal access to the polls.[42]

Since the 1910s, white Methodist women had been working with African American women, Methodist and non, to ensure equal rights before the law. They listened to African Americans about what they wanted and needed instead of just assuming that because they were white, they knew the answers to everyone's problems. Methodist women who were members of the Woman's Division supported, petitioned, and wrote anti-lynching, desegregation, and voting legislation. They supported various forms of nonviolent protests, such as the sit-in. They didn't let social critique or ridicule stop them from spreading what they believed to be the true message of Jesus—the equality of all before God and therefore before the law. With the 1964 Civil Rights Act, the 1965 Voting Rights Act, and the dissolution of the Central Jurisdiction in 1968, it seemed that the Woman's Division could finally celebrate and relax. However, they continued to work toward building relationships among diverse people because they knew that, through relationship building, equitable understandings of each other's natural place beside one another would emerge. Their fights continued through various new organizations within The United Methodist Church: the Commission on the Status and Role of Women, Black Methodists for Church Renewal, and the Commission on Religion and Race. Through these organizations, their witness would continue to be heard and continue to bring real, political and social change. Nevertheless, they preached.

41 Knotts, *Fellowship of Love*, 226.
42 Knotts, 227.

Discussion Questions

1. Have you ever participated in a march or protest for a cause? What did you learn from that experience?
2. How does your local church advocate for racial equity? How can it improve in its advocacy for racial equity?
3. What resources from the General Commission on Religion and Race might you use in your local congregation?
4. How might your local congregation engage your local branch of #BlackLivesMatter to embrace racial equity?

THREE: THE EQUAL RIGHTS AMENDMENT

If we keep on this way they will be celebrating the 150th anniversary of the 1848 Convention without being much further advanced in equal rights than we are. . . . If we had not concentrated on the Federal Amendment we should be working today for suffrage. . . . We shall not be safe until the principle of equal rights is written into the framework of our government.

—Alice Paul

All over the country women in local churches, in annual conferences and at theological seminaries were talking to one another and making plans, changing themselves and the institutions around them.

—Elaine Magalis, *Conduct Becoming to a Woman*

In 1973, Elaine Magalis wrote *Conduct Becoming to a Woman*, a history of Methodist women struggling for ordination and finding religious authority in mission. In her own words, the book was meant "to communicate something of the struggle of the forebears of the present-day churchwoman—and perhaps to help her gain new perspectives on her own life and work." Hopefully it would "give her some sense of her own history (or herstory), some feeling for her beginnings."[1] The first two chapters of this book have endeavored to lay out some of that "herstory." We've seen Methodist women lead the fight for suffrage, for ordination, and for racial equity. However, when it came to supporting the Equal Rights Amendment (ERA), Methodist women took a few decades to support such a change. It was only after other advances in women's equality were made that Methodist women felt the amendment was fully necessary and best for all women. This chapter will detail the steps needed to progress women's equality and representation forward within the Methodist tradition in order for them to support the Equal Rights Amendment (ERA) in 1972.

Why did it take Methodist women so long to get on board with the ERA? Writing two years after the ERA was passed by the United States Congress and while it was being ratified state by state, Magalis surprisingly spent little time discussing the ERA in her *Conduct Becoming to a Woman*. It's only in the last few pages that the ERA is mentioned, but it is also here that she gives us a hint as to why Methodist women weren't originally supportive of the ERA.

> One moral and social issue that was also a woman's issue was the Equal Rights Amendment. Year after year it failed to come to a vote in the U.S. Congress, and year after year it was denounced in social policy resolutions handed down by the woman's organizations. They would favor passage only with one very important qualification: that protective laws for women not be jettisoned by it. But by 1971 when the Equal Rights Amendment finally came to a vote, women's groups, including United Methodist women, were adamantly opposed to any qualification to the Amendment; they no longer wanted "protection."[2]

Magalis points out some of the obstacles to passing the ERA. For years, women were taught by men that they needed to be protected from society: they were weaker, more passive, frail, and thus they could never seek equality because it meant overlooking these "natural" qualities of woman.

---

1   Elaine Magalis, *Conduct Becoming to a Woman: Bolted Doors and Burgeoning Missions* (New York: Women's Division, Board of Global Ministries, The United Methodist Church, 1973), v. Magalis wrote the book as part of a mission study for the seventy-three annual conferences published by the Women's Division. A study guide, "Women over Half the Earth's People," was used with the Magalis book. Hundreds of United Methodist women across the country were involved in the study in Schools of Christian Mission and in local churches in 1973.

2   Magalis, 130.

Magalis found that even within Methodist circles in the 1970s, girls were still being taught this: "A 1970 study of United Methodist nursery school curriculum found that girls are actually taught 'to be helpless, frightened, passive, waiting and weak.' They need protection. Women expect it for themselves; society expects it for them."[3] These qualities of womanhood have a long and deep history in the United States and Western world, and they led to the creation of what historians call the "cult of true womanhood" and the "ideology of separate spheres." These phrases describe hegemonic constructions of femininity that women were expected to uphold that, in reality, ensured their subordination to men during the eighteenth and nineteenth centuries, a time when women had limited access to education, legal rights, property rights, and professional opportunities. Magalis recognized that these qualities that created the "image of 'the lady'" had been "modified" over time but only in a few ways. The core that created this pious, weak, frail image of a "lady" was essentially "unchanged" in the 1970s, as "both men and women act[ed] as if it were a scientifically established fact of nature instead of a cultural myth."[4]

In her book, Magalis provided an alternate narrative for churchwomen, one that showcased how through mission work women found ways to assert their voice and fight for their rights. Magalis argued that within missionary organizations such as the Methodist Protestant Woman's Foreign Missionary Society, "the spirit of 'Woman's Rights' not only 'lurked' in the women's societies—it was a robust and lively presence."[5] This was evident through the ways these women worked to dismantle patriarchal systems, which kept women and girls from achieving greatness in other parts of the world. For example, one missionary, Isabella Thoburn, focused her work on educating women and girls in India. She began a girls' school, Lal Bagh, in 1871 and the first Christian woman's college in Asia that same year. Magalis claims that these schools and others like them "change[d] the almost universal opinion of the inferiority of [the female] sex."[6] Beyond education, these missionary women fought to change child-marriage laws so that girls under a certain age could not be married, as well as laws that forbade women being cared for by male doctors. Many women were reluctant to go to a doctor knowing that doctors were only male; thus, changing the laws to allow women to see women doctors would've encouraged more women to seek medical

---

3   Magalis, 130.
4   Magalis, 130.
5   Magalis, 24.
6   Magalis, 59.

attention when needed. The work that women were able to do in the twentieth century relied on the rhetoric and work of women in the nineteenth century. It was easy to argue in the 1970s that the ERA was a necessary addition to the US Constitution in order to recognize the full dignity of women, because Methodist women had been making this argument for women in other countries for more than one hundred years.

The Women's Caucus, the Women's Division, and the Committee on Women's Concerns joined forces to help United Methodist women understand what it meant to be a churchgoing woman in the 1970s. Their main efforts were aimed at helping women understand how the concept of "lady" and the "conduct becoming to a lady" had changed due to women's efforts to change social constructs. They argued that women who were educated to their potential as human beings, citizens, and Christians would naturally find that they had a large role to play in society and in the church. For "women, with a vision of whole persons, whole church, and whole Christians, will continue to face down prejudice to create a system of conduct *becoming to a woman*!"[7] From lady to woman, Methodist women set out to change their futures and their place. Magalis's goal throughout her book is to show that the myth can change when women set out with the explicit mindset to change it.

Churchwomen's Liberation

With the creation of The United Methodist Church (The UMC) in 1968, the Woman's Division of the Methodist Church was combined with women's organizations from the Evangelical United Brethren to create the Women's Division of the Board of Missions (later changed to Board of Global Ministries). The Women's Division carried on the mission of the Woman's Division in seeking to create more equitable opportunities for witness and ministry within the church and within American society at large. Around 1970, the Women's Division made this more explicit when they created an ad hoc Churchwomen's Liberation committee to financially support churchwomen who participated in efforts to build a more inclusive society. According to Magalis, "All over the country women in local churches, in annual conferences and at theological seminaries were talking to one another and making plans, changing themselves and the institutions around them." Churchwomen's Liberation financially supported "groups to plan women's studies in curricula in seminaries; women's centers to offer counseling, child care,

---

7   Magalis, 133, emphasis original.

or other aids to women's students; research groups; and teams working to transform theological understandings of whole bureaucracies that traditionally have been cast in masculine terms."[8] Primarily focused on educating other women about their equality and removing barriers such as childcare that so often prevented that education, the Churchwomen's Liberation committee spent their time on "consciousness raising," exposing women to even the idea that in God's eyes they were equal to men. Women were taught that if we, as good Christians, wanted God's kingdom to be here and now, then we had to make claims of equality to men here and now. The committee helped women understand what it was to be a woman in the 1970s and to understand how pervasive male domination was in society. The official Committee on Churchwomen's Liberation was created in 1970 with a mandate that included "continu[ing] exploration on the issues of women's liberation," including the development of "criteria" for "funding of projects."[9]

By 1973, the Committee on Women's Concerns described its own work as "consciousness raising about women's issues," which included using "various resources out of the women's liberation movement as a basis for discussion" as well as preparing "resources on churchwomen's liberation for United Methodist Women (articles in *Response*, packets, etc.)." The committee thus continued the work of previous women's organizations by increasing women's self-awareness through education. They also reported having worked to increase "full participation of women in the decision making [process] of the total church, especially General Conference and other legislative groups." One of the best ways to ensure that women's concerns are heard is to ensure that women have not only a voice but a vote, and participation at General Conference was vital to that process within The UMC. The idea of "churchwomen's liberation" was multifaceted. It was meant to speak to women's ability to be active leaders within their local church and general church contexts and to speak to the need for more women active in the clergy and even episcopacy of the denomination. It was also meant to speak to churchwomen's need to carry the message of equality out of the church, to society at large. According to Kirby, "This concept embodied the particular history and strategies relevant to women in the church whose secular sisters were carefully, although sometimes stridently, articulating the conditions of society that perpetuated discrimination against women." Women had to face a harsh reality: "on one hand . . . the leaders and history of the Christian

---

8 Magalis, 131.
9 Ellen Kirby, *The Evolution of a Focus: Women's Concerns in the Women's Division, 1970–1980* (New York: Women's Division, 1983), 7.

tradition were exceedingly patriarchal and male dominated; on the other hand there existed the message of equality, freedom and liberation as seen in the themes of the tradition (e.g. exile and Exodus) and in the life and teachings of Jesus Christ."[10] Methodist women were called to bridge this divide, to overcome the patriarchal leadership and history, and to bring the message of equality to the forefront of the conversation.

This breach between a patriarchal past and an equitable future caused many women to leave the institutional church, believing it too ingrained in male domination to be fixed. Others stayed in and fought for change from within, to make the church the headlights for women's liberation in an increasingly dark society. For, nevertheless, these women preached. They joined seminaries and pursued a theological education in numbers previously not seen. Seminaries responded by creating departments centered on a theology of women's liberation. Some denominations saw the demise of their women-centered organizations; others, like The UMC, witnessed the rise of multiple women-centered and women-led organizations. This is what made Methodism unique; its response to the women's liberation movement was not to flee, but to embrace. This embrace was solely due to the centuries of work of Methodist women who worked tirelessly to ensure women's equality and racial equality.

But Methodist women did more than simply make women part of the conversation; they actively supported women in their efforts to educate themselves and make their voices heard. In the 1960s, the Women's Division sponsored "two scholarship funds for women seminary students," and in the 1970s, "a scholarship fund of $10,000 was set" to ensure that financial constraints would not prevent women from attaining seminary education.[11] Between 1970 and 1973, the Women's Division "contributed nearly $30,000 . . . in the form of small grants (ranging from $500 to $3,500) to groups of women working toward the elimination of discrimination against women in seminaries and other institutions of theological education, toward projects which are offering creative alternatives to meet the needs of women, and toward new approaches in ministry by women." Finally, the committee also recognized early on the privilege of white women in the women's liberation movement and continued the ministry of the Woman's Division work toward racial equity by focusing on the participation and representation of "minority

---

10 Kirby, 6–7.
11 Kirby, 7. In the 1970s seminary was not nearly as expensive as it is today, so $10,000 would have funded multiple women's educations.

ethnic women" and "the development of minority group leadership in the organization of United Methodist Women."[12]

Crucial to helping women understand themselves as equal was reframing the theological conversation. In 1971, the Committee on Churchwomen's Liberation set aside $5,000 "to enable a gathering of women from across the country to share ideas and strategies around the emerging issues and questions of feminist theology." Peggy Billings, chief of staff of the Section of Christian Social Relations, brought to the Women's Division "a strong concern for lay women's participation in theology." Women needed to better understand the falsity of Christian tradition's patriarchal systems and language. If the cult of true womanhood and the qualities of being a "lady" were somehow rooted in the Bible, then women needed to use the Bible to correct these false assumptions.

Bringing liberation theology to the everyday laywoman was a necessary first step. In 1973, the first "Woman Exploring Theology" conference was held, sponsored by the ecumenical group Church Women United. One participant in this program, Dr. Audrey Sorrento, remembered the impact of this first conference: "Through much discussion, clarification, and difficulty, our group was able to agree and to present a new model for understanding God." This new model was expressed thusly: "God *creates.* God *participates* in humanity in the person of Jesus Christ. God *energizes* with the Spirit. God is complete with the *grounding* of humanity." She concluded that when one person "extend[s] [their] creative function, [they] touch other people's circles of completeness. If they participate in my creation and I in theirs, we have community."[13] In other words, when we recognize ourselves as women, as whole beings, and when we have an understanding of God that is based in community (as opposed to hierarchy), we are more likely to be able to make a difference in this world. Kirby explains the impact of Women Exploring Theology: "This [conference] shows how from a vertical model, using male-centered language, we moved to non-sexist language and, more importantly, expanded our understanding of God as personal, as social, and as related to humanity."[14]

Despite its best intentions, the Women Exploring Theology conference did not have the impact on laywomen that it hoped. It was still too erudite and only catered to women interested in pursuing postgraduate theological education. To respond to this continued lack of engagement with everyday

---

12 Kirby, 7–8.
13 Kirby, 18.
14 Kirby, 19.

laywomen, the United Methodist Women (UMW) produced *The Ongoing Journey: Women and the Bible*, a mission study book that endeavored to help women better understand their new roles, questions, and experiences as women in the 1970s through the eyes of women of the Bible.[15]

The work of this committee and of the Women's Division during the 1970s is outlined by Ellen Kirby in her book, *The Evolution of a Focus: Women's Concerns in the Women's Division, 1970–1980*. As an employee of the Women's Division during this time, Kirby dedicated most of her professional life to the liberation of women-at-large. In the early part of her twenty-year career with the Women's Division, Kirby primarily focused on women's concerns within United Methodist Women, membership, and interpretation of the organization's mission. She was tasked with helping the Women's Division respond to changes women experienced in their daily lives in the 1970s. Kirby was also involved with a wider range of issues, including peace, racism, global justice, and environmental concerns. Through her work on women's concerns, Kirby set out to speak to those women about their place in the church and in society.

She argues that throughout the 1960s women within the Methodist Church were increasingly being pushed aside, despite their recent gain of full ordination rights in 1956. The Woman's Division was reorganized within the Board of Missions, resulting in a restriction of their work, budget, and reports. However, women had proven their worth and their ability to enact political change in the recent civil rights and peace movements. In universities and seminaries, women were increasingly being exposed to liberal theology, which advanced notions of women's equality in the eyes of God. And in society at large, women were taking on new, more public roles. Thus, with the formation of The UMC in 1968, it was prime time that the denomination created a completely separate organization for women, and they did. In fact, they created two.

1972 General Conference

The 1972 General Conference is often remembered, especially by more progressive-leaning United Methodists, as a scarred conference for its creation of the infamous "incompatibility clause," which claimed "the practice of homosexuality" was "incompatible with Christian teaching." While this amendment has created great harm for LGBTQIA individuals within and outside The UMC, the 1972 General Conference did have some redeeming

---

15 Kirby, 19.

moments. Meeting in Atlanta, Georgia, the 1972 Conference was "a turn-ing point for work on women's concerns." In these two weeks, the General Conference formally organized two major women's organizations (United Methodist Women and the Commission on the Status and Role of Women), formed the General Board of Global Ministries, recognized the work of the Women's Caucus, and passed a resolution that declared United Methodist support of the Equal Rights Amendment.[16]

The Commission on the Status and Role of Women (COSROW) was cre-ated in 1972; and in 1973, the Women's Societies of Christian Service and the Wesleyan Service Guild combined to form United Methodist Women (UMW). In 1944, Mrs. Bragg, the Woman's Division president, analyzed the *Discipline* and found "widespread discrimination and lack of opportunity for women in the church," an early reference to the "stained-glass ceiling" effect, which will be detailed in chapter 5. The study became the focus of a widely popular Woman's Division National Seminar in 1947. This, in turn, led to a 1967 Woman's Division petition to the 1968 General Conference "for a general church study on the role of women in the church." In 1970, the general church "set up the mechanism for a study commission which orga-nized in 1970 and brought a report to the 1972 General Conference." The newly formed Women's Caucus then promoted a petition in 1972 that, with the support of the Women's Division, argued for "an ongoing commission." Thus, in 1972, COSROW was created as a permanent commission that held the "responsibility of fostering an awareness of problems and issues related to status and role of women with special reference to full participation in the total life of the Church."[17]

The new UMW was designed "to attract a younger and more plural-istic membership, including the increasing numbers of women employed outside the home" for "its image and identity needed to keep up with the expanding, changing roles of women."[18] The two organizations were cre-ated for very different reasons. COSROW is a commission of the general church, as opposed to a membership organization, and it focuses more on general church structures, providing resources for the church-at-large, and ensuring that women are represented and respected throughout all levels of the church. (Note that also in 1972, the Commission on Religion and Race was created to ensure that racial equity is asserted and maintained through-out all levels of the church.) UMW, however, is a membership and mission

---

16 Kirby, 10.
17 Kirby, 10.
18 Kirby, 6.

organization that centers on public policy as part of its mission. One of the primary ways it connects its members to public policy is through "Action Alerts," many of which are cited throughout the remainder of this book.

The UMW is one of the largest organizations of churchwomen worldwide. In a recent conversation with Ellen Kirby, I asked her whether there was something unique to United Methodism (or Methodism in general) or to Methodist women that propelled their ability to use their faith to act politically. She responded that "the Methodist tradition is rooted in ministry and mission to the needs of the world and the most oppressed among us." Going back to Wesley, "his ministry embodied social holiness," and thus, "within this context, Methodist women were historically bound to serve their neighbors at home and abroad." The introductory chapter of this book has laid out this exact argument. Kirby added that there was also something unique about the organization, United Methodist Women, and its ability to connect women at different levels of the organization—from the local church, to the annual conference, to the agency level, and from missionaries, to deaconesses, to ministers, to laywomen. It created these connections across time, space, place, class, race, and ability and allowed United Methodist women to use their voices in a new way. In her book, Kirby claims, "Certainly the largest number of churchwomen working for ratification of the Equal Rights Amendment could be found among United Methodist Women."[19]

With these new organizations and resolutions, at the 1972 General Conference, "women were visible as never before" in the life of the church. A mere 13 percent of the delegates were women at this General Conference, and they were trained by UMW concerning women's issues during General Conference. At each General Conference since 1970 (even before the creation of these more official organizations), UMW and COSROW have held women's orientation sessions to ensure that women are not only present but heard at General Conference and to ensure that they are aware of the logistical processes (e.g., *Robert's Rules of Order*).[20]

Equal Rights Amendment

The Equal Rights Amendment was written rather quickly after women gained suffrage in 1920. Alice Paul, suffragist and early women's rights activist, knew that the right to vote would not guarantee women full equality before the law; for that, women would have to be explicitly named as equal in the US

---

19 Kirby, 6.
20 Kirby, 11.

Constitution in order to protect them fully from sex discrimination. This led her to pen the original amendment in 1923 at the seventy-fifth celebration of the Seneca Falls Convention. It originally read, "Men and women shall have equal rights throughout the United States and every place subject to its jurisdiction." In 1943, she changed the wording to "Equality of rights under the law shall not be denied or abridged by the United States or by any state on account of sex."[21]

Methodist women began to support the ERA in the early 1970s, primarily through the lobbying and educational efforts of the Woman's/Women's Division, the same organization that joined and led civil rights demonstrations and sought to dismantle the Central Jurisdiction in the MEC, as detailed in chapter 2. Since the 1940s, the Woman's Division had supported legislation geared toward equal pay for equal work. Much to their dismay, those efforts are still underway today. Before 1971, the Women's Division (and its predecessor, the Woman's Division) had considered the ERA but didn't support it. Thelma Stevens, longtime staff and head of the Christian Social Action of the Women's Division, affirms that the Woman's Division officially considered the ERA twice, once in the 1940s and once in the 1950s. With its focus on women's working rights, the Women's Division did not support the earlier versions. Essentially, women before the 1960s worked in very different conditions than did men, and thus they needed special protections on the job. They more often worked in cotton mills or as domestic workers. In the eyes of the Woman's Division, seeking equal working conditions might take away some of the special protections afforded to women, given their dangerous work environment. However, the Woman's Division did fight for "achieving equality in wages, job opportunities, and safe working conditions" before 1970.

When the ERA was rewritten in 1970, the protections afforded to working women had become a burden on women's ability to progress in their professional careers, and thus the time was ripe for support. In 1971, "the Women's Division Executive Committee unanimously approved support for ratification of the E.R.A. and joined a host of other national organizations urging Congressional support."[22] With the concerted efforts of the Women's Division and the General Board of Church and Society, the 1972 General Conference "voted almost unanimously to urge United Methodists to be

21 ERA.org, "History of the Equal Rights Amendment, accessed February 18, 2020, https://www.equalrightsamendment.org/the-equal-rights-amendment.

22 Kirby, *The Evolution of a Focus,* 20; GCAH folder "Women's Division Endorses Equal Rights Amendment, February 17," 1971. United Methodist Communications.

involved in the ratification efforts in their respective states," and thus the 1972 General Conference officially endorsed the amendment.[23]

Rather quickly thereafter, by 1973 anti-ERA forces were beginning their work within the denomination and Methodist women were countering this through more overt efforts to ensure its ratification. On February 9, 1973, a "night" letter was distributed to United Methodist agency presidents, to chairs of the UMW and Women's Society for Christian Service, and to members of the Wesleyan Service Guild in states where the ERA had not yet been ratified. Written by Joyce Hamlin of the Committee on Women's Concern of the Women's Division, it read: "We are on the threshold of a historical event—ratification of Equal Rights Amendment to the Constitution . . . Both Women's Division and General Conference voted support for this amendment which guarantees equal rights for men and women."[24] It ensured that those reading the letters knew that they lived in a state where the ERA had not yet been ratified and cautioned that anti-ERA "organizations" were "working actively for defeat in key states." The "night" letter recommended "joining efforts of groups such as Business and Professional Women, N.O.W., and American Association of University Women for ratification." Sixty-nine copies of the letter were sent to various leaders of women's organizations within The UMC.[25]

Enclosed with the letter was a packet on the ERA that included specific actions that would help women move from communication to political action. The Women's Division was evidencing how they didn't just educate and inform women but told them how to be politically active. First, the women were encouraged to "call the office of your state legislator and find out when the ERA is to be voted on in your state." Second, they were to "urge letters and wires in support of the ERA to state legislators." Third, readers were told, "Adopt a resolution from your executive in support of the ERA, including the United Methodist Church position on it, and send a press release of the action to as many local papers as possible." Also included was a pamphlet entitled "How and Why to Ratify the Equal Rights Amendment," published by the National Federation of Business and Professional Women's Club. It explained what the ERA was, how it would become law, why it was needed, and who supported it. It made the case that "yes," the ERA is really needed for "the fact that persistent patterns of sex discrimination continue to permeate our social, cultural, and economic life" despite the "progress . . . in recent years." The pamphlet contended that the Fourteenth Amendment

---

23 Kirby, *The Evolution of a Focus*, 20–21.
24 "United Methodist Information," February 13, 1973. GCAH 2165-5-1-7.
25 "Night Letter," February 9, 1973. GCAH 2165-5-1-7.

wasn't enough, for it places the burden of proof on women to show that sex discrimination is unreasonable instead of guaranteeing protection altogether. It then addressed the fears that anti-ERA parties were spreading regarding how the ERA would negatively affect women: for instance, by including them in a military draft, removing protection laws of laboring women, setting quotas that limit how many women can attend school, upsetting the social or familial relationships between men and women, depicting men and women as identical, forcing men and women to sleep in the same dormitory rooms or use the same restrooms, removing maternity benefits, disrupting homemaking by removing women from the home, or disallowing rape as a criminal punishment.[26]

The UMC quickly made its own version of this pamphlet, entitled "The Church, Religion, and the Equal Rights Amendment." It made many of the same arguments and used similar rhetoric, often focusing its arguments on the very fears pronounced by anti-ERA strategists. However, it also included statements from various denominations, including The UMC, advertising wide religious support for the amendment.

Despite their best efforts, the anti-ERA factions continued to gain traction. Thus, in February 1976, the Religious Committee for the ERA was organized with the hope of making "more visible" those "religious organizations" that supported the ERA to secure its ratification by 1979.[27] It was made up of twenty-two members and was an interfaith coalition of Catholic, Jewish, and Protestant organizations. Its leaders felt that the support of religious organizations had been underreported. Nancy Fifield McConnell of the UM Board of Church and Society stated:

> Support of ERA is a logical action based on our Judeo-Christian heritage
> which stresses equal responsibility. . . . Equality of men and women
> is affirmed in the first chapter of Genesis and examples of leadership
> by women are found throughout the Old Testament. The New Testa-
> ment further develops the concept of equality of men and women. Jesus
> repeatedly rejected prevailing customs and treated women as persons
> of equal worth.[28]

Pro-ERA women had to base their arguments in scripture because anti-ERA groups were basing theirs in scripture. This was not the first time the Bible had been used as a weapon or rhetorical tool to disprove another

---

26 "How and Why to Ratify the Equal Rights Amendment," GCAH 2165-5-1-7.

27 Initial work to form the group began three months before, in December 1975.

28 "Why a Religious Committee for the Equal Rights Amendment?" GCAH 1481-1-7-6.

side, and it would definitely not be the last. Anti-ERA advocates argued that
the amendment would "destro[y] the family and femininity, promot[e] anti-
Americanism, and violat[e] the will of God."[29] Statements such as this were
circulated widely. Another read:

> The ERA, both on the state and federal levels, could in essence make
> Christianity illegal and force conservative Christians to choose between
> obeying clear teaching from the Holy Bible or laws of government which
> are contrary to the authority of the Holy Bible. . . . [T]he ERA could con-
> ceivably declare Biblical Christianity unconstitutional and be instrumen-
> tal in destroying our family structure, which is so deeply rooted in the
> Hebrew-Christian Scriptures and traditions![30]

These types of arguments assumed that to be Christian you had to believe
that men and women were not in fact equal but were differently created
creatures meant to occupy complementary (not equal) roles. This was
somehow divinely ordained when woman was created out of man and
when woman was punished after the fall and made obedient to man. As
these types of arguments were made, individual religious opposition to the
amendment increased while religious organizations support of the amendment also increased.

By 1976 about thirty religious organizations openly supported the ERA
and joined the Religious Committee for the ERA. Its members believed that
"the dignity of personhood has been bestowed equally on all individuals,
both female and male, by our Creator." And "as long as inequality under the
law exists, the fullness of our humanity under God has not been realized."[31]
Women and men working together and working equally could "produce
greater accomplishment toward wholeness and justice in the social, economic, and political life of our nation."[32]

With arguments like these based in scripture, these women set out to
"organize and mobilize for action." They encouraged women and men to
"write, visit, sign petitions, and cooperate with state coalitions" to ensure the

---

29 "Why a Religious Committee for the Equal Rights Amendment?"
30 "Why a Religious Committee for the Equal Rights Amendment?"
31 United States Congress Senate Committee on the Judiciary, Subcommittee on the
    Constitution, *Equal Rights Amendment Extension: Hearings Before the Subcommit-
    tee on the Constitution of the Committee on the Judiciary, United States Senate,
    Ninety-fifth Congress, Second Session, on S.J. Res. 134 . . . August 2, 3, and 4, 1978*
    (U.S. Government Printing Office, 1979), 292.
32 Equal Rights Amendment, quoted in Board of Church and Society, United Methodist
    Church, *Engage/Social Action* 6 (1978).

ERA's passage. By 1976, thirty-four states had ratified the ERA; four more states were needed.[33] The efforts of the late 1970s and early 1980s show an intense, highly organized, and overtly political campaign on behalf of Methodist (and non-Methodist) women to ensure ratification. Arguments for the equality and dignity of all of humanity were based in scripture and were voiced by women active in women's organizations of their respective faiths.

In 1976 and 1980, the General Conference of The UMC continued its support for the ratification of the ERA as well. In 1976, the Conference supported a resolution entitled, "Equal Rights of Women," which began, "The Gospel makes it clear that Jesus regarded women and men as being of equal worth. Nowhere is it recorded that Jesus treated women in a different manner than he did men."[34] It continued to further evidence how Jesus included women in his ministry: "Biblical evidence indicated that others, including women, were considered to be disciples or followers of Jesus. In open defiance of the customs of his society, Jesus taught women, spoke to them in public, refused to accept the idea that childbearing was a woman's most important function. Moreover, women were the first witnesses to the Resurrection and were directed to go and tell their brothers."[35] Going directly against the anti-ERA interpretations of scripture, this resolution declared that other "interpretations" were keen to "unduly" emphasize "male superiority." Using references to the original Hebrew, it disproved the argument that women were created as inferior "helpers" and instead argued that the original word used in Gen 2:18 had no connotation of inferiority but was meant as a symbiotic understanding of help. The resolution situates The UMC's support of the ERA within its own "historical concern for justice, human dignity, and equality for every person." After providing statistics about how many states still needed to ratify, the resolution called "current attitudes toward women in the United States blatantly discriminatory, based on stereotyped ideas of a woman's abilities and proper roles in society, rather than on her actual potential and rights as an individual."[36]

To directly counter the anti-ERA arguments that the ERA would negatively affect family life, the Board of Church and Society produced multiple pamphlets outlining how it would actually affect family life. The first, written by Charles V. Petty, was called "ERA and Family Life."[37] Petty argued that

---

33 Namely, Illinois, Missouri, North Carolina, and Florida.
34 Board of Church and Society, "Equal Rights of Women," 1976, GCAH 2218-4-5-28.
35 Board of Church and Society.
36 Board of Church and Society.
37 Charles V. Petty, "ERA and Family Life," Board of Church and Society, GCAH 2218-4-5-28: ERA 1977.

"the impact of the ERA on familial stability" or instability "will not be that significant" because the ERA would in no way force women to work outside of the home, nor would it affect "traditional" gender roles. His pamphlet directly countered the argument that the ERA would undermine "Christian teachings relative to the family," similar to the one discussed earlier. Petty claimed that these arguments are based primarily in "forms" and not "principles." By "forms," Petty meant that anti-ERA parties contend that our families today should look exactly like those of Adam and Eve, and Abraham and Sarah—that is if you ignore the fact that Abraham raped his slave, Hagar. Petty argues that a better way to understand Christian tradition in regard to family is to look at the principles of family life—"love, faithfulness trust, support, oneness, respect, kindness, gentleness, goodness, patience, forgiveness, submission, discipline, etc."[38] Upholding principles prevents people from upholding specific texts that are often taken out of context.

The second pamphlet countering the anti-ERA cluster, written by Ellen Kirby of the Women's Division, was entitled "ERA: For the Sake of the Family." It was originally printed in the *Christian Home* but was quickly reproduced as a brochure by the General Board of Church and Society. She begins by arguing that "a fundamental element of the Christian faith is commitment to social justice," and this commitment is "biblically based," for it "is part of God's ongoing revelation for our lives." Kirby uses "specific facts" to "provide evidence of injustice and discrimination." First, at the time, women earned "a little over half the median wage for men." Second, "44 percent of divorced mothers are awarded child support." Third, discriminations continued in "credit transactions," which often prevented mothers, widowers, or single women from being able to open charge accounts. Fourth, "inheritance laws" often discriminated against widows. Kirby then moved on to other, more emotional forms of discrimination. For instance, domestic violence was considered a civil offense, not a criminal one. Kirby argued that rather than undermining the family, the ERA would "strengthen family ties since it establishes a legal climate that affirms the full personhood of women." Women would be seen as more than "domestic servants" who were "mental[ly] incompetent." They could work outside the home if they chose to, but they would never be forced to. The ERA would allow all to function as "effective individuals" who contribute uniquely and equally to the survival and maintenance of the family life in whatever way they choose.[39]

---

38 Ellen Kirby, "ERA: For the Sake of the Family," Board of Church and Society, GCAH 2218-4-5-28: ERA 1977.

39 Kirby, "ERA: For the Sake of the Family."

Thirty states quickly ratified the ERA, but the efforts were stopped short through the work of a fundamentalist woman, Phyllis Schlafly, who spread "fear and misinformation" surrounding what the ERA would do to "woman-hood" in American society. Schlafly and her anti-ERA campaign influenced burgeoning conservative and fundamentalist caucus groups within The UMC, including Good News (and its *Good News* magazine) and the Institute for Religion and Democracy (a far-right political group that sought to undermine theological liberalism in all mainline Protestant denominations). However, the General Conferences of 1976 and 1980 continued to "overwhelmingly" support resolutions that promoted ratification of the ERA.[40]

In fact, the ERA "became the symbol of the Women's Division's strong support for women's equality." American religious historian Martin E. Marty described the incredible support of United Methodists for the ERA (as opposed to other major Christian groups). "The United Methodists," he stated, "are also strong in states reluctant to ratify." He continued:

> Their national General Conference has supported E.R.A. since 1972, and most regional and local boards and bureaus have spoken up for it. The leadership of the 1.2 million member Women's Division recently asked their fellow Methodists, to avoid vacationing in these slow to ratify states. . . . Equal rights for women commands a lower priority than equal rights for racial minorities did. Cautious or numbed, most church people seem to cherish the sidelines, while Methodist women advocate selective tourism.[41]

The work of the Women's Division was primarily focused in those states that still needed to ratify the amendment. Using a similar tactic employed during the civil rights movement, they asked Methodist women to not vacation in states that refused to ratify. In 1977, the Women's Division decided that it would only hold its national meetings in states that had ratified the ERA, again echoing their previous meetings only being held in nonsegregated states.[42] It was through these small acts of protest that most Methodist women felt they could find their public and political voice. They didn't have to go out of their way to be active in the movement; they could be active through their absence.

---

40 Board of Church and Society, "Equal Rights of Women," 1976.
41 Martin E. Marty, "Confusion Among the Faithful," *Saturday Review,* as quoted in Kirby, *The Evolution of a Focus,* 21.
42 Kirby, 24.

The Women's Division worked directly with the General Board of Church and Society on a joint project called the "ERA Support Project." It had an advisory staff and directors representing both agencies, and it produced resources such as pamphlets and films to inform everyday women and correct the ubiquitous misinformation promoted by Schlafly. The Women's Division was also a founding member of E.R.A. America, of which it was the only religious group on the board.

As the 1970s came to a close and the United States became more involved in the Vietnam War, women's fears of being part of the draft quickly closed any progress on the ratification of the ERA. Even though only three states were needed for ratification, all efforts were essentially stalled. However, despite this loss, many women, through their newly found public and political voices working to ratify and garner support for the ERA, were elected to state legislatures. Ecumenical relationships had been established that would continue to fight for not only women's equality but equality across the board.

As of 2020, the ERA has yet to be passed. The time for ratification has officially expired, and yet if the three necessary states did ratify it, it might force the conversation in Congress and could potentially lead to an official amendment to the US Constitution. Between 1995 and 2016, various state legislatures brought up the ERA for ratification but failed to gain the approval of both houses. However, on March 22, 2017, Nevada became the thirty-sixth state; on May 30, 2018, Illinois became the thirty-seventh; and on January 15, 2020, Virginia became the thirty-eighth state to ratify the ERA.[43] We must now wait to see when or if the conversation will be brought up in both the House and Senate.

Ironically, since 1988, The United Methodist Church has sought to amend its own constitution to include gender as a protected status. In 2016, the General Conference finally voted to approve this amendment, and it passed with a two-thirds majority. The language supported would add ability, gender, age, and marital status to the protected identities of paragraph 4, article 4. It would then read:

In The United Methodist Church, no conference or other organizational unit of the Church shall be structured so as to exclude any member or constituent body of the Church because of race, color, national origin, ability or economic condition, nor shall any member be denied access

---

43 Timothy Williams, "Virginia Approves the E.R.A, Becoming the 38th State to Back It," *New York Times*, January 16, 2020), https://www.nytimes.com/2020/01/15/us/era-virginia-vote.html.

to an equal place in the life, worship, and governance of the Church because of race, color, gender, national origin, ability, age, marital status, or economic condition.[44]

Following a similar process to the United States government, the amendment then must be ratified by two-thirds of the aggregate annual conference membership. Over the next twelve months, the amendment went to each annual conference for a vote, and it failed to pass, receiving only 61 percent affirmative votes. Equality before the law is a continuous fight for women everywhere—in governments around the world, in the public sphere, and in the church. I conclude this chapter with the following reflection from the Reverend Leigh Goodrich on the failure of the UMC amendment:

> In a world in which #MeToo is worldwide phenomenon; in a world in which women continue to make significantly less for doing the same work as men; in a world in which women are bullied on the streets and in churches, the General Commission on the Status and Role of Women will seek to provide protection for women worldwide who seek membership in The United Methodist Church. The outcome of the ratification of this amendment has not dissuaded, but rather, energized members of annual conferences to take action on women's equality issues. It is with that energy that we still work for the full and equal participation of women in The United Methodist Church.[45]

Discussion Questions

1. Has the state where you live ratified the ERA? If not, what can you and your local congregation do to ensure that it is ratified?
2. How might the ratification of the ERA affect your daily life?
3. Do you experience gender oppression on a daily basis?
4. How does your local congregation work to support women, both lay and clergy?
5. How does your local congregation work to support women outside of your congregation?

---

44 Leigh Goodrich, "Paragraph 4, Article 4 Breakdown," General Commission on the Status and Role of Women, accessed February 18, 2020, https://gcsrw.org /MonitoringHistory/WomenByTheNumbers/tabid/891/post/paragraph-4-article -4-vote-breakdown/Default.aspx.
45 Goodrich.

FOUR: REPRODUCTIVE RIGHTS

> [United Methodists have a] sacred responsibility to plan when and how many children to have and guard women's right to access comprehensive reproductive health care, including the ability to end a pregnancy legally and safely when necessary.
>
> —United Methodist Women

In the 1960s American Methodism, in terms of social policy, was at its most radical. During this decade, American Methodists rewrote their sexual ethic, favoring Christian guidelines for sexual decision-making over rigid rules that deemed certain acts good and others bad. By the end of the 1960s, some Methodists supported the gay rights movement through the founding of the Commission on Religion and the Homosexual, an organization that brought together interfaith leaders and gay rights activists in cities across America to fight for equal (or at least more civil) treatment of gay communities. Other Methodists were cofounders of the Clergy Consultation Service on Abortion (CCSA), an organization that counseled women considering an abortion and referred them to a licensed doctor who was willing to perform the service in a safe and sterile environment. This chapter will detail Methodist support of women's reproductive rights beginning with the CCSA, through the Religious Coalition for Abortion Rights (RCAR), and up to now.

The importance of the CCSA cannot be overstated. Founded in 1967 by Rev. Howard Moody (American Baptist) and Rev. Finley Schaef (Methodist), the CCSA sought to address not only the lack of access to abortion but also the stigma surrounding it. The CCSA was an interfaith effort, bringing together twenty-one Protestant ministers and rabbis in New York City. The group's purpose was "not to encourage abortions but to offer compassion and to increase the freedom of women with problem pregnancies."[1] Surprisingly, and unlike the other chapters of this book, this story starts off with Methodist men. It was male ordained Methodist clergy who began the conversation about reproductive rights within the Methodist tradition by the late 1960s. This is not to say that Methodist women were not having these conversations or seeking to gain full reproductive rights. But in terms of recorded and public conversations or statements, the first seem to be from male Methodist clergy. Once that conversation began, however, Methodist women, primarily through their newly established women's organizations (COSROW, UMW, and Women's Division) quickly stepped in to continue the fight in the early 1970s.

Abortion in the Nineteenth Century

To talk about abortion today and why access to abortion is critical, it is important to go back and examine why abortion became illegal in the 1870s, why it became legal again in the 1970s, and why its access has been increasingly limited since *Roe*. In the latter half of the nineteenth century, women began using homemade contraceptives at a surprisingly effective rate. Articles on how to make contraceptives or prevent conception were readily available in the 1860s and 1870s through marital advice guides, newspaper advertisements, and almanacs, and actual contraceptive products were for sale in local stores. Contraceptive use had become so rampant in the 1870s that certain parties began to organize and argue for its immorality. One man, Anthony Comstock, was especially poignant in this argument. By 1873, the US Congress had passed what are colloquially called the "Comstock laws," which banned the use of contraceptives and the distribution of contraceptive information through the US postal service.[2]

Without access to information or devices to prevent conception, women turned more and more toward abortion, a postconception remedy to an

---

1   Edward B. Fiske, "Clergymen Offer Abortion Advice," *New York Times*, May 22, 1967.
2   John D'Emilio and Estelle B. Freedman, *Intimate Matters: A History of Sexuality in America*, 3rd ed. (Chicago: Univ. of Chicago Press, 2012), 60.

unwanted or problematic pregnancy. Many women, especially in rural areas, relied on oral tradition to induce a miscarriage. Included in this oral tradition was a mix of effective and ineffective means: drinking mixtures of roots and herbs, bleeding from the foot, hot baths, jumping repeatedly, douching, and (arguably the least effective) rubbing gunpowder on your breasts while drinking a tea made from rusty-nail water.[3] More invasive procedures were also used. For example, women would insert various probes into each other's vaginas, hoping to induce miscarriage. More often than not, these attempts resulted in tears and punctures, which often led to infection and death.

One constant about abortion has been the secrecy of it. Women in the 1860s and '70s who chose abortions seldom spoke of it. In contrast to contraception, which was more openly discussed, abortion was rarely spoken of or written about. Largely those who sought abortions during this time were white, working and middle-class, single and married women. After the 1870s, more married women began to seek abortions than single women. Few women left written records of their abortions, but estimates from reformers claim that between 1800 and 1830 there was one abortion for every twenty-five to thirty live births. By the 1850s, there was one abortion for every five to six live births. This increase is most likely due to married women seeking to limit family size instead of single women seeking abortions. By 1878, a report from the Michigan Board of Health estimated that "one third of all pregnancies in [Michigan] ended in abortion, and that seventy to eighty percent were secured by 'prosperous and otherwise respectable married women.'"[4]

During this time, abortion was not illegal even if it was something not often discussed. The practices were rarely condemned as long as they were conducted early on in the pregnancy. Most doctors, clergy, and women understood that "life" didn't begin until the woman felt movement of the fetus, a time known as "quickening," generally understood to occur between sixteen and twenty weeks of gestation. Between 1820 and 1840 the first abortion laws were passed. These laws regulated abortion according to quickening and were meant to protect women from being forced to receive an abortion, not to prosecute them for acquiring one. Laws became more stringent between 1860 and 1890 as forty states rejected quickening as the window for the procedure and began limiting advertisements for abortion services. These moves transferred the decision from the pregnant woman

---

3   D'Emilio and Freedman, 63.
4   D'Emilio and Freedman, 65.

to the doctor.[5] The new laws coincided with the professionalization of the medical industry. They directly targeted and undermined the knowledge of midwives (one of the main providers of abortions) in lieu of the medical education of professional physicians.[6]

The ban on contraception and the new laws limiting abortion access did not mean that women no longer used contraception or chose abortion. It did mean, however, that only women of a certain economic status or with certain overseas connections had access to effective contraception and safe abortions. Instead of ridding the country of what Anthony Comstock deemed "obscene," the Comstock laws and the laws limiting abortion merely made contraception and abortion elite items, only available to white women of a higher socioeconomic class. It left lower-class and working-class women, who were predominantly African American or immigrant, with few, life-threatening options.

Abortion in the Twentieth Century

By the 1920s, largely through the lobbying efforts of birth control advocate and reformer Margaret Sanger, most Protestant clergy and Jewish rabbis had accepted that contraceptive use was acceptable to their faiths as long as it was done within marriage. This reflected a growing trend, especially among middle-class families, of smaller family sizes. Essentially by the late 1920s, most middle-class families had found ways around the bans on contraception and abortion to successfully limit their families to two or three children.[7] Families with fewer economic means and less social capital had a very different story. Thus, by the 1920s, Protestants were endorsing access to contraception and abortion to alleviate poverty.[8] The Methodist Episcopal Church endorsed contraceptive use by 1928, and the Methodist Church endorsed the use of contraception within a marriage by 1940.[9]

---

5   D'Emilio and Freedman, 66.

6   R. Marie Griffith, *Moral Combat: How Sex Divided American Christians and Fractured American Politics* (New York: Basic Books, 2017), 207.

7   D'Emilio and Freedman, *Intimate Matters,* 174.

8   For more on Protestant clergy's involvement in early reproductive rights, see Tom Davis, *Sacred Work: Planned Parenthood and Its Clergy Alliances* (New Brunswick, NJ: Rutgers Univ. Press, 2004). For more on Methodist involvement in early reproductive rights, see Ashley Boggan Dreff, *Entangled: A History of American Methodism, Politics, and Sexuality* (Nashville: New Room Books, 2018).

9   Dreff, *Entangled,* 34-60.

By the 1950s, contraception was promoted more and more to married couples. However, contraception was not always effective, either due to the product itself or to user error. Therefore, abortion became the last resort, and in the mid-twentieth century abortion was still sought after. Margaret Sanger studied access to abortion in the 1920s and found that one in five pregnancies was intentionally terminated. Women who had had one abortion were more likely to have a second or third. Two decades later, Alfred Kinsey reported that 22 percent of his surveyed married couples had sought an abortion. In his survey of single women, most women who became pregnant while single sought an abortion. In the mid-1950s, the director of Planned Parenthood estimated that "roughly 2,000 a day, every day—are performed in the United States." She believed that most of these were performed on married women who had other children.[10]

Even though abortion seemed to be widespread within the US by the mid-1950s, access to an abortion in a hospital setting was becoming harder and harder to obtain. Many states by 1960 had outlawed all but "therapeutic abortion," which was allowed only if pregnancy threatened the life of the mother. Even with these restrictions, the number of therapeutic abortions performed in hospitals dropped dramatically in the 1940s and 1950s for a number of reasons. First, women were required to petition a hospital board to receive a therapeutic abortion. If granted a hearing, they were then asked to explain, in person, alongside a doctor who recommended the procedure, how the pregnancy threatened their life. If the board granted their request, then they had to find a doctor willing to perform it. In these hearings, the most commonly cited threat to life was psychiatric. Most hospitals at the time had a quota of the number of therapeutic abortions it would allow for a set term. Many hospitals had a policy requiring women who received a therapeutic abortion to also be sterilized, adding additional and unnecessary trauma to an already traumatic experience.[11]

Some abortion providers operated outside of hospital regulations in small family practices. One family practice doctor in eastern Pennsylvania estimated that he had performed more than twenty-eight thousand abortions in his career. However, most women in the 1950s and 1960s obtained abortions from unlicensed professionals (either in the hospital or in small family practice) in "back alleys." These women obtained information on how to get an abortion by word of mouth. One reported, "You had to ask around. You asked friends and they asked friends, and the ripples of asking people

---

10 D'Emilio and Freedman, *Intimate Matters,* 252–53.
11 D'Emilio and Freedman, 253.

widened until some person whose face you might never see gave over the secret information that could save you." One constant since the 1870s was that married women with economic and social means could obtain this information faster and more reliably than women of lesser means.[12] Historians John D'Emilio and Estelle B. Freedman argue, "Without doubt, America had experienced a contraceptive revolution in the twentieth century, but for many women the revolution offered little in way of autonomy. As voluntary family planning through contraceptive practice became the middle-class ideal, those social groups which remained outside the consensus were targeted by regulatory agencies seeking to impose the new norm."[13]

By the late 1960s, women involved in the second wave of feminism recognized that full control of their reproductive systems was vital to attaining full equality. Thanks to innovations in contraception, such as the 1961 advent of the contraceptive pill, many barriers to controlling their own reproductive lives had been removed.[14] However, abortion was still criminalized by the 1870s laws. During the 1960s many states loosened some restrictions on abortion. Doctors, rather than hospital boards, were given some room to recommend abortions. But feminists in the 1960s recast abortion not as a medical issue but as a rights issues, the right to control one's own body.[15]

The Clergy Consultation Service on Abortion

Clergy had been involved in discussions regarding women's reproductive rights since the 1920s, when Margaret Sanger came to them for support of the birth control movement. Ministers have sat on the board of the Birth Control Federation of America, later renamed Planned Parenthood Federation of America, since its founding. In the 1940s, there was a national clergyman's advisory council to the federation whose first proclamation was signed by 480 Protestant and Jewish clergy from forty-three different states.[16] Methodist bishops, most prominently Bishop Oxnam, served on this advisory board and openly advocated for women to have greater control over their

---

12 D'Emilio and Freedman, 254.

13 D'Emilio and Freedman, 255.

14 For more on the invention of the contraceptive pill and how it drastically changed the conversation regarding women's reproductive health, see John Eig, *The Birth of the Pill: How Four Crusaders Reinvented Sex and Launched a Revolution* (New York: W. W. Norton, 2015); and Elaine Tyler May, *America and the Pill: A History of Promise, Peril, and Liberation* (New York: Basic Books, 2011).

15 D'Emilio and Freedman, *Intimate Matters,* 315.

16 Griffith, *Moral Combat,* 209; Davis, *Sacred Work,* 55–56.

reproductive lives.[17] Therefore, clergy advocating for women's reproductive rights was not new or surprising. Clergy had made similar arguments and had participated in comparable conversations and advocacy efforts for four decades. Clergy who supported women's access to full reproductive rights focused their message on the liberating power of faith. Those of the Christian faith argued that "the true message of Christianity was love for others and liberation from the tyranny of unjust rulers, whether reigning over church or state."[18] What could be more unjust or tyrannical than not having control over what happens to one's own body?

Thus, those who were paying attention to clerical advocacy might not have been surprised by the May 22, 1967, article on the front page of the *New York Times*, which announced the founding of the Clergy Consultation Service on Abortion (CCSA). The brainchild of Rev. Howard Moody of Judson Memorial Baptist Church and Rev. Finley Schaef of Washington Square Methodist Church, the CCSA was born naturally out of ongoing conversations among clergy serving in the Greenwich Village area of New York City. An ecumenical council of about twelve clergy members had been meeting at Washington Square Methodist Church, "talking about theology and social issues and that sort of thing, and one of the social issues was abortion."[19] Thanks to the work of historians Doris Andrea Dirks and Patricia A. Relf, there is now a comprehensive history of the CCSA. The history recorded here relies heavily on the information they provide in *To Offer Compassion: A History of the Clergy Consultation Service on Abortion.*

Reverend Schaef was newly appointed to serve Washington Square in 1966. Under his leadership, the church became a center for resistance to the Vietnam War for the Greenwich Village area. It was a frequent host of protests, counseling, and assistance to those who resisted the draft. As Schaef remembers, the idea to convene the CCSA for the purpose of making referrals was his. He and Moody had both had experiences with trying to connect women in need of an abortion with a safe and reliable provider. For Shaef, the person in need of an abortion was a young girl who was raped by her stepfather. Unable to find the girl help, Schaef determined that something had to be done, and clergy were the ones who should step up.[20] Another Methodist clergyman involved in the CCSA early on was Rev. Jesse

17 Dreff, *Entangled.*
18 Griffith, *Moral Combat*, 206.
19 Doris Andrea Dirks and Patricia A. Relf, *To Offer Compassion: A History of the Clergy Consultation Service on Abortion* (Madison: Univ. of Wisconsin Press, 2019), 23–24.
20 Dirks and Relf, 24.

Lyons, who served at Riverside Church in the Upper West Side of Manhattan.[21] Reverend Lyons also had personal experience with abortion, as his niece contracted rubella while pregnant and gave birth to a child with severe disabilities as a result of not being allowed to get an abortion.[22] Personal stories such as this are why clergy easily supported the efforts and goals of the CCSA.

The organizing efforts began quickly after the initial conversations between Shaef and Moody. A small group of ministers gathered at Washington Square to educate themselves on abortion. They dove into the medical and legal sides of the procedure and discussed how they might establish a referral service. Clergy wanted to know what a woman in need of an abortion had to go through. They also wanted to know what women experienced during the procedure and what medical information they needed to provide to abortion servicers. So, they brought in women who openly admitted to having had an abortion to hear directly from them what it was like. One woman described her terrible experience of meeting someone she didn't know in a parking lot at midnight to be escorted to an unknown location where the procedure would be performed. The uncertainty and secrecy made her experience more anxiety inducing and traumatic than it already was or needed to be. The clergy also heard from doctors who were licensed abortionists. They described in detail exactly what happens during an abortion and which steps might be painful for women. Clergy also consulted with lawyers to learn how close to breaking the law they might come. Lawyers never told clergy that they would not be arrested for making referrals; after all, abortion was illegal, and providing means to an abortion was thus abetting a crime. The consequences for making referrals could be a fine or even jail time. Lawyers offered ways to help circumvent laws, including only referring women to physicians out of state, advice that would become the staple of other Clergy Consultation Services chapters as they spread across the country.[23] Clergy were also advised to be open about their referrals. If it looked like a secretive endeavor, then it would be more suspicious. Instead, clergy were quite open with their willingness to offer referrals (hence the announcement on the front page of the *New York Times*) and relied legally on their duty to confidentially counsel women on spiritual and moral matters. Finally, clergy were told they should never handle any of the financial

---

21 Dirks and Relf, 24.
22 Dirks and Relf, 24.
23 Dirks and Relf, 25–26.

exchanges between women and providers. All such exchanges should happen elsewhere and be handled by the women themselves.[24]

After educating themselves and receiving various consultations from women, doctors, and lawyers, the clergy took the next step in organizing. Reverend Moody was chosen as the spokesperson, and Judson Memorial as the base of the organization. The group settled on their name, specifically on openly incorporating the word *abortion* in the name, with the hope that it would help to normalize the word. Using euphemistic words or phrases such as *problem pregnancy* might not reach all the women in need of an abortion. However, as the organization spread across the country, other CCS organizations would use euphemistic words depending on their location, demographic, and state laws.[25]

Finally, the group wrote and released a statement of purpose, which read:

> The present abortion laws require over a million women in the United States each year to seek illegal abortions which often cause severe mental anguish, physical suffering, and unnecessary death of women. These laws also compel the birth of unwanted, unloved, and often deformed children; yet a truly humane society is one in which the birth of a child is an occasion for genuine celebration, not the imposition of a penalty or punishment upon the mother. These laws brand, as criminals, wives and mothers who are often driven as helpless victims to desperate acts. In the meantime, women are being driven alone and afraid into the underworld of criminality or the dangerous practice of self-induced abortion. Therefore, believing as clergymen that there are higher laws and moral obligations transcending legal codes, we believe that it is our pastoral responsibility and religious duty to give aid and assistance to all women with problem pregnancies. To that end we are establishing a Clergymen's Consultation Service on Abortion which will include referral to the best available medical advice and aid to women in need.[26]

These clergy made it clear that women who could not access abortion were unfairly punished and subjected to the penalty of carrying an unwanted pregnancy and raising an unwanted child. As clergy, it was their moral and pastoral duty to work to change the law when those laws unfairly targeted groups, preventing them from living their full life. It was their religious duty to assist women in need so that they might thrive.

---

24 Dirks and Relf, 26.
25 Dirks and Relf, 28.
26 Dirks and Relf, 28–29.

The logistics of the CCSA were established. Women would call the listed number and be sent straight to an answering machine. The machine provided the numbers of clergy who took turns being on call each week. Those who called weren't expected to leave a message. Instead, they were expected to choose a clergyperson based on denomination or location and call the number provided. Little information was exchanged over the phone; instead, an in-person counseling appointment was set.

In the first week after the opening statement ran in the newspaper, the CCSA "was deluged with calls, including many from across the country and some from clergy wanting to set up services in their own regions."[27] Rabbi Buz Bogage was on call the first day and recorded receiving thirty-five calls that first day, with four to five of those callers identifying as Catholic and 60 percent as Jewish. This number did not include calls that went to the other two clergy on call that first day, or those women who called the operation without following up with a call to a listed clergyperson.

Like Margaret Sanger, who pushed clergy in the 1920s to openly and actively support contraception, author and abortion activist Larry Lader pushed Moody, Schaef, and others to be proactive with abortion referrals. Lader knew that clergy speaking openly and positively about the moral necessity of women having access to abortion would open the conversation up in new ways and bring it more into the public light.[28] Clergy talking about abortion would destigmatize it.

The ministers involved in the initial efforts of the CCSA were heavily influenced by the various rights movements of the 1960s, which all sought to challenge laws that prevented people from living into their full personhood. These ministers continuously witnessed young women in crisis, unable to fully determine the future of their own bodies. For them, it was "unconscionable that women who had gotten pregnant out of wedlock faced the choice between having their lives ruined by an 'illegitimate' child and risking the dangers of an illegal abortion."[29] It was also well-known after the CCSA opened that it wasn't only women who became pregnant out of wedlock who sought abortions. Abortions were necessary across the board, for contraception at the time, if available or accessible to a woman, was not always reliable. These ministers were further astounded at the forced sterilization of lower-income and African American women and that these two groups were

---

27 Dirks and Relf, 31.

28 Dirks and Relf, 21–22.

29 Daniel K. Williams, *Defenders of the Unborn: The Pro-Life Movement before* Roe v. Wade (New York: Oxford Univ. Press, 2019), 65.

at a higher risk of dying from an illegal abortion or self-abortion attempt. Thus, the only valid, moral, and Christian-minded thing to do was to try in some way to connect women with safe abortions.

The United Methodist Church and Abortion

Within The United Methodist Church, the conversation regarding abortion was brought to the General Conference primarily through activists within the CCSA and the Women's Division, but it wasn't framed as a women's rights issue. In 1970, during the special session of the General Conference, The UMC endorsed abortion "upon request" by a substantial majority but within the context of population control.[30] It was believed that controlling the quickly expanding population of the world was a moral necessity, for an uncontrolled population increase disadvantaged the poor more than it did the wealthy. Overpopulation threatened all nations and brought with it "mass starvation" and "depletion of natural resources." To combat this, the resolution stated that The UMC supported "the small family norm" and took "the lead in eliminating those hospital administrative restrictions on voluntary sterilization and abortion."[31] With this, all UM hospitals were to grant an abortion to all women who wanted one in order to keep their families small and thus contribute less to overpopulation. The resolution further called on the federal government to "remove the regulation on abortion from the criminal code" and make it available "only upon request of the person most directly concerned." Approved by an "overwhelming majority," the purpose of this original 1970 statement was to prevent children from being born "to suffer and to experience despair."[32]

However, once the conversation surrounding the morality of abortion became more public, especially in the lead-up to *Roe*, this overwhelming endorsement of abortion had already begun to waver by 1972. An evangelical-leaning caucus called the Good News movement, created in 1967, began lobbying General Conference to bring United Methodism back to its "evangelical" roots. According to Good News president and founder Rev. Charles Keysor, United Methodism had been catering to culture instead of being models of scriptural Christianity. After 1972, Reverend Keysor would use abortion and the rights and status of gay and lesbian people to garner

---

30 "Population Crisis," *Book of Resolutions of The United Methodist Church* (Nashville: United Methodist Publishing House, 1970), 17–18.
31 "Population Crisis," 17–18.
32 "Population Crisis," 20.

support for his conservative evangelical caucus—and he was quite successful in doing so.

Within two years, the 1970 statement was amended in a variety of
ways. First it was moved from the *Book of Resolutions* to the *Book of Discipline*. It was no longer associated with the population crisis but was instead
moved to a paragraph entitled "Birth and Death." These two switches alone
signal the seriousness with which United Methodists were discussing abortion. While the *Book of Resolutions* carries weight, it does not carry the
same weight as the *Book of Discipline*. Further, we see a shift in the rhetoric
around abortion; no longer is it considered a solution to the population
crisis, thus making it a moral choice to better the world. Now it is associated with a conversation about life and death, showcasing the influence of
the larger, pro-life argument on the conversation. By 1972, United Methodists recognized a fetus as "unborn human life" and were "reluctant to
approve abortion." However, after this initial sentence, the statement moves
toward a more proabortion access stance that centers on the sacredness of
the mother's life and well-being "for whom devastating damage may result
from an unacceptable pregnancy." In the end, United Methodists called for
a "prayerful inquiry" by those who seek abortions, the "removal of abortion
from the criminal code," and "thorough and thoughtful consideration by the
parties involved, with medical and pastoral consent."[33] This statement still
supports a woman's right to an abortion if she chooses; it still supports the
legalization of abortion in 1973. However, its opening line and its approval
only after medical and pastoral consent signaled to those who identified as
pro-life United Methodists that the conversation was shifting.

With this subtle shift in 1972, abortion became one of the more talked-
about issues between the two groups throughout the remainder of the
1970s until now. *Good News* magazine ran articles that were pro-life in substance, that aimed to provide a biblical basis for life beginning at conception,
and that sought to convince United Methodists that abortion was immoral.

In 1973, the Supreme Court of the United States legalized abortion.
In the decision of *Roe v. Wade*, it was determined that up until the fetus is
viable outside of the womb, women, in consultation with their physician,
had a legal right to access abortion. Thus, access was granted during the first
trimester and made more easily available during the second trimester. Five
months before *Roe*, a Gallup poll reported that "two out of three Americans
think abortion should be a matter for decision solely between a woman and

---

33 "Birth and Death," "Social Principles," *Book of Discipline of The United Methodist
Church* (Nashville: United Methodist Publishing House, 1972), 86.

her physician." In this same survey, 64 percent of Americans supported the "full liberalization of abortion laws," an all-time high in America.[34]

However, the fight to provide *all* women with actual access to abortions did not end with the ruling of *Roe v. Wade*. The CCSA in New York and most of its related branches across the United States closed their doors after *Roe,* believing their work of referrals was no longer necessary. However, it soon became apparent that another organization needed to be formed to protect women's now-legal right to an abortion. This effort was picked up by Methodist women, largely the women of the General Board of Church and Society, United Methodist Women, and the Women's Division. In 1973, women from these United Methodist organizations worked with other religious organizations to found the Religious Coalition for Abortion Rights (RCAR). Working with Methodist clergy and bishops alongside Jewish and other Christian clergy, their goal was to ensure that a proabortion access voice was present in an increasingly religiously framed conversation, one that would be a counterpoint to a side that was calling itself "pro-life" and was determined to limit women's access to abortion based on the religious understanding that life begins at conception.[35]

The RCAR worked primarily through education, awareness, and lobbying. They wrote and disseminated pamphlets detailing the science and medicine behind the abortion procedure, spoke from a clerical lens in favor of the morality of abortion, and provided testimony of women who had either attempted abortions when they were illegal or were currently in dire need of an abortion and unable to secure one. The RCAR worked to protect abortion clinics and ensure the safety of those entering and those working. Some of their more visible, and thus controversial, work was in lobbying the United States Congress to maintain abortion access for all.[36]

In 1976, Theresa Hoover, associate general secretary of the Women's Division and national sponsor of RCAR, testified to Congress against the Human Life Amendment, one of the many proposals that sought to undo or restrict *Roe*. According to Hoover, RCAR had "a unique character" in that it was constructed of various religious groups, all of whom approached the morality of abortion differently but who all believed that "every woman should have the legal choice with respect to abortion, consistent with sound medical practice

---

34 Griffith, *Moral Combat,* 201.
35 Dreff, *Entangled,* 185–89.
36 Dreff, *Entangled,* 185–89.

and in accordance with her conscience and religious beliefs."[37] Hoover relied on the First Amendment in her argument to Congress, "It must be emphasized that our opposition to the proposed constitutional amendments stems from the recognition that the question most basic to the abortion debate is the question of when life begins. We believe this to be above all a theological question on which each denomination or faith group must be permitted to establish and follow its own teachings but *must not* be allowed to impose them through law on society at large."[38] Using the religious freedom language of the First Amendment, Hoover centers the question of abortion not on a woman's reproductive rights but on her religious rights. She has the right, in consultation with her clergy or spiritual advisor, to determine when life began according to her own faith. This switch in rhetoric helped RCAR use the same rhetoric the pro-life campaigns used—the idea that abortion was a moral and religious choice—but RCAR used it to say that one religion, one denomination, or one faith group could not impose their religiously motivated definition of when life begins on society at large. Thus, women who were of a faith that believed that life began at conception had the right to not access abortion. However, women who were of a faith that believed life began when a fetus is viable outside of the womb or with its first breath outside of the womb also had an equal right to access abortion legally.

In her role as a spokesperson for RCAR, Hoover represented various faith groups, including The UMC. Other United Methodists by the mid-1970s had quickly joined in the abortion debate, trying to figure out if abortion access was a woman's right or a moral choice. The General Board of Church and Society and the Women's Division worked with RCAR to produce educational materials that argued that abortion was not talked about in scripture, that it was a moral choice that women could make with a sound heart and mind, and that life did not begin at conception according to Methodist theology.

One of the main United Methodist publications to come out of the pro-access side was a booklet titled *Abortion: A Human Choice*.[39] It offered

---

37 "Statement of the Religious Coalition for Abortion Rights before the Subcommittee on Civil and Constitutional Rights of the Committee of the Judiciary U.S. House of Representatives" (March 24, 1976), GCAH folder "Religious Coalition for Abortion Rights 1979," Women's Division, 2593-7-6:1, 2.

38 "Statement of the Religious Coalition," 3, emphasis in original.

39 Board of Christian Social Concerns of The United Methodist Church, *Abortion: A Human Choice*, Division of General Welfare, Department of Population Problems, May 1971, 5; GCAH folder "Abortion Packet 1972," administrative records of the Division of General Welfare of the General Board of Church and Society.

an ethical, theological, and legal guide to United Methodists who were con-
flicted on the morality of abortion. One of its contributing authors was Rev.
Tilda Norberg, an ordained clergywoman in New York who had previously
worked for CCSA. Reverend Norberg's article "Female Anguish and Abortion" shared the stories of women who sought abortions, most likely gathered from her days working for the CCSA. She told of a fifteen-year-old girl
whose parents believed that the only "humane way out of an already emo-
tionally damaging situation" was to have an abortion; an African American
woman who finally found the courage to divorce an abusive husband only
to learn that she was pregnant by him; a forty-five-year-old woman whose
last of four children had just gone to college and was looking forward to the
opportunity to self-improve only to learn that she was again pregnant; and
a woman with four children, all under the age of seven, whose husband's
income could barely cover their current expenses.[40] These stories showed
the variety of women who had sought abortions and their situations and
reasons for doing so. From girls to married women to battered women, all
women deserved the right to end an unwanted pregnancy. Reverend Norberg's evidence gathered while working for the CCSA showed her that most
women who sought abortion were married. She provided further evidence
that women who were unable to obtain a wanted abortion had children with
more mental health issues and problems adjusting to society than children
who were welcomed into a family.

Through the work of the General Board of Church and Society and the
Women's Division, the General Conference of 1976 supported abortion in
a new resolution, "Responsible Parenthood." It stated that the continuation
of a pregnancy that endangered the life or health of a mother was "not a
moral necessity." It further read, "We believe the path of mature Christian
judgment may indicate the advisability of abortion; we support the legal right
to abortion as established" by *Roe*. Finally, it admitted that it was ultimately
a woman's choice: "We encourage women in counsel with husbands, doctors, and pastors to make their own responsible decisions concerning the
personal and moral questions surrounding the issue of abortion."[41] The
"Responsible Parenthood" resolution would be upheld by each General
Conference until 2016, when it was not supported and thus removed from
the *Book of Resolutions*.

---

40 Tilda Norberg, "Female Anguish and Abortion," from *Abortion: A Human Choice*.
41 "Responsible Parenthood," *Book of Resolutions of The United Methodist Church*
     (Nashville: United Methodist Publishing House, 1976).

The abortion paragraph in the *Book of Discipline* was amended slightly between 1972 and 1984. But in 1988, through the lobbying efforts of Good News, a new sentence was added: "We cannot affirm abortion as an acceptable means of birth control." This amendment might seem like a small change in rhetoric, but it makes a judgment on the rationale of many women and undermines their ability to have "mature Christian judgment" when it comes to whether or not to have a child.

After 1988, the evangelical pro-life voice within The UMC only grew stronger. In 1991, evangelical pro-life United Methodists wrote and released "the Durham Declaration." Organized by the Taskforce of United Methodists on Abortion and Sexuality (also known as Lifewatch), nine United Methodist pastors and laypersons gathered together and wrote this document focused on "abortion-prevention." The declaration called the church to a "scriptural, theological, and pastoral approach to abortion," as if the General Conference's calls to "mature Christian judgment" and "council with . . . pastors" was not a scriptural, theological, or pastoral approach. The declaration names a fetus as a "child . . . created in the image of God and . . . for whom the Son of God died." Using this rhetoric, it claims that the "life of this child is not ours to take" and that it is "a sin to take this child's life for reasons whether of birth control, gender selection, convenience, or avoidance of embarrassment."[42] Ignoring the fact that women often chose abortion for reasons beyond these listed, there is no theological underpinning or scriptural backing for the statement that unborn fetuses are children created in the image of God.

With the advent of Lifewatch's and Good News' support of the Durham Declaration, the two groups used General Conference 1992 to target United Methodist involvement with and support of RCAR. The groups rallied to try to get The UMC to withdraw its membership from the organization. In 1992, United Methodists voted to retain their membership in RCAR, but only by a margin of thirty-seven votes. At every General Conference since the vote on whether or not to maintain membership with RCAR (after 1993 called the Religious Coalition for Reproductive Choice) has been close. General Conference voted to leave the organization in 2016, the same General Conference that voted to no longer support the resolution titled "Responsible Parenthood."[43]

---

42 Lifewatch, "The Durham Declaration," accessed February 17, 2020, https://www .lifewatch.org/the-durham-declaration.html.

43 Susan Henry Crowe and Harriett Jane Olsen, "An Open Letter to the Religious Coalition for Reproductive Choice," United Methodist Women, June 7, 2016, accessed December 1, 2019, https://www.unitedmethodistwomen.org/news/letter-to-the -religious-coalition-for-reproductive-choice.

Since 1972, the *Book of Discipline*'s statement on abortion has gone from a few lines in a paragraph entitled "Birth and Death" to its own paragraph, entitled "Abortion," which spans one and a half pages. Currently, the paragraph reads as a mixed bag of pro-life and pro-access phrases. It still upholds the "sanctity of unborn human life[, which] makes us reluctant to approve abortion." It still encourages Methodists "to respect the sacredness of the life and well-being of the mother." It still supports "the legal option of abortion under proper medical procedures" but also puts limitation on that right in statements against abortion as "birth control," for "gender selection or eugenics," and for "late-term abortions." Newer language asks the church to help provide services and education to work to prevent pregnancy in the first place through "comprehensive, age-appropriate sexuality education, advocacy in regard to contraception, and support of initiatives that enhance the quality of life for all women around the globe."[44]

Abortion Today in The United Methodist Church

In 2016, the removal of the "Responsible Parenthood" resolution and the withdrawal from RCRC was problematic for The UMC. Since the 1920s, Methodists have been at the forefront of the fight for women to have full reproductive control of their lives. "Full reproductive control" includes the right to access abortion, but it is not limited to abortion. Reproductive rights involve a whole host of topics that are outside of abortion: basic knowledge of a woman's reproductive system, sexual education, family planning education, contraceptive access and education, and education about menstruation and menopause, breast cancer, pelvic screening and PAP smears, and yes, abortion. The goal of RCRC was never to promote abortion. The goal of the Women's Division and the General Board of Church and Society was never to promote abortion. The goal of the "Responsible Parenthood" resolution was never to promote abortion. These various organizations' and statements' goal was to ensure that women were educated and had access to contraception and comprehensive healthcare, and that when these failed, they still had a choice to end an unintended or problematic pregnancy.

After General Conference 2016, United Methodist Women issued a statement that helped bring much-needed clarity to the intention of the "Responsible Parenthood" resolution: "[It] upheld the church's affirmation of families' sacred responsibility to plan when and how many children to

---

44 *Book of Discipline of The United Methodist Church*, 2016 (Nashville: United Methodist Publishing House, 2016), ¶161, p. 115.

have and guarded women's right to access comprehensive reproductive health care, including the ability to end a pregnancy legally and safely when necessary."[45] It continued to state that the resolution "challenged the gender inequality that leaves many women in the world with little or no say in their own health care decisions."[46] In their statement, UMW addressed the misinformation that claims that reproductive health care is a code word for abortion. Correcting this, they stated that "women's reproductive health is central to women's total health care throughout the childbearing years and beyond, for as women age the reproductive system becomes more at risk for disease." The statement also corrects the misinformation that the resolution was at odds with the statement on abortion in the *Book of Discipline*. Instead, UMW states, the "resolution detailed how to fulfill the church's call within its abortion statement to reduce unintended pregnancies and to support initiatives that enhance the quality of life for women and girls. Comprehensive reproductive health education, care and nutrition, and unfettered access to contraception are essentials for accomplishing these stated goals." Their statement concluded by mentioning that the resolution had broadened its language in recent years to be more globally minded to the situation of women and girls worldwide: "It brought to light the harsh realities of life for women and girls around the world, including child marriage, spousal disapproval, lack of access, legal restrictions, gender inequality, and financial barriers, all of which limit women's access to safe contraception."[47] This expanded call to address systemic inequality of women worldwide lives into the gospel's assertion that Jesus valued all women and children, especially those who were marginalized by systemic injustices.

The 2016 General Conference of The UMC voted to withdraw from the RCRC by a wide margin: 425 to 268. The UMC was not officially a member, but two of its organizations—the General Board of Church and Society and United Methodist Women—were. Given the typically close nature of votes surrounding matters of human sexuality, this wide margin evidences an increasingly pro-life denomination. As votes on the rights and status of lesbian and gay people in The UMC grew closer and closer, the votes on abortion grew further and further apart. While these organizations were

---

45 United Methodist Women, "The Church Still Supports Women's Reproductive Health, but We Have Work to Do," https://www.unitedmethodistwomen.org/news/the-church-still-supports-womens-reproductive-health.

46 United Methodist Women.

47 United Methodist Women.

forced to withdraw their support, five annual conferences of The UMC joined the RCRC independently: Oregon-Idaho, California-Nevada, New England, New York, and Pacific Northwest.[48] These conferences wanted to publicly show their support of RCRC and their disapproval of the denomination's withdrawal. After the General Conference vote, Rev. Dr. Susan Henry Crowe, general secretary of the General Board of Church and Society, stated, "Faith voices must speak up for women who are vulnerable. Our voice has been removed from the table of the Religious Coalition for Reproductive Choice (RCRC)—a coalition comprised of partners from many faiths dedicated to women's health—but we will continue to speak up for women and girls." In a similar manner, Harriet Jane Olsen, top executive of United Methodist Women, stated, "We really can't talk about women's health without talking about reproductive health. Abortion is just one procedure available for one part of a women's life cycle. It is tiny in comparison to the whole need of women's health."[49] Both of these women see abortion as a small part of what RCRC does, while the pro-life wing of United Methodists understands RCRC as a lobbying group that only lobbies for abortion access.

Abortion Today in the United States

Since General Conference 2016, Donald J. Trump has been elected as president of the United States. His nominations to the United States Supreme Court (SCOTUS) have resulted in a majority conservative shift. In 2019, after the confirmation of Brett Kavanagh to the Supreme Court, Georgia, Alabama, Mississippi, Louisiana, Utah, Arkansas, Kentucky, Missouri, and Ohio have all sought to further limit women's legal access to abortion in hopes of overturning *Roe*. While these new laws have yet to go fully into effect, and many of them will make their way through various courts up to the Supreme Court, they were passed in order to test SCOTUS on the current legality of abortion. *Roe* established that a woman had a right to seek an abortion up until the fetus was "viable" outside of the womb, between twenty-four and twenty-eight weeks of pregnancy. Before 2019, there was no state law on the books that banned abortion before twenty weeks.

48 Kathy L. Gilbert, "5 Conferences Join Faith Coalition on Reproductive Rights, Abortion," *United Methodist News Service*, June 22, 2016, https://www.umnews.org/en/news/oregon-idaho-takes-up-support-for-rcrc-denied-at-gc2016.

49 Gilbert.

Instead, states have worked to limit abortion through limiting women's access to abortion providers. Clinics that provide the service have been shut down, resulting in women having to take time off work and travel perhaps hundreds of miles to a clinic. Eighteen states require mandatory counseling to women seeking abortions. Included in this counseling are unproven scare tactics that link abortions to breast cancer, the ability of a fetus to feel pain, or the long-term mental health consequences a woman will face after seeking an abortion. Twenty-seven states require a waiting period, between twenty-four and forty-eight hours from the time a woman requests an abortion to the time the procedure is performed, resulting in women having to take time additional time off work or pay extra traveling expenses to follow through with the procedure. Thirty-seven states require parental consent for minors, twenty-six of which require both parents to consent.[50] These various restrictions have resulted in women not being able to fully access their legal rights. These hurdles have worked to effectively make abortion unavailable to the majority of women. They have re-created the pre-*Roe* problem of only women of a certain financial means with familial support to exercise their legal right to control their own bodies. Women of lesser economic means, girls who have been raped by their fathers or other family members, women in abusive relationships, women without supportive employment, and a whole host of other unique and tragic situations have resulted in tens of thousands of women losing their rights to access abortion.

However, if a woman could successfully navigate the above restrictions, she could still obtain an abortion until the twentieth week. That is, until 2019. These 2019 bans are different in that they seek to ban abortions before twenty weeks. Alabama aims to outlaw and criminalize abortion—period. No abortions will be granted in the state after conception. It has exceptions if the woman's life is threatened, but it does not allow exceptions for rape or incest. Arkansas and Utah would not allow an abortion after eighteen weeks but would still allow exceptions for cases involving rape, incest, or medical emergencies (in Utah, a police report must be filed). Passing "heartbeat bills," Georgia, Kentucky, Louisiana, Mississippi, and Ohio would ban abortions after six weeks—before many women even know they are pregnant. Only one of these bans allows for exceptions for rape or incest, and only if a police report is filed (Georgia), while the others follow Alabama's lead in not allowing for an exception for rape or incest. Missouri would ban abortion

---

50 Guttmacher Institute, "An Overview of Abortion Laws," accessed December 1, 2019, https://www.guttmacher.org/state-policy/explore/overview-abortion-laws.

after eight weeks, with no exceptions for rape or incest. All of these bans still allow for an abortion if the woman's life is endangered.[51] To counter this trend, New York, Vermont, and Illinois have worked to increase abortion access. These three states reaffirmed a woman's legal right to access an abortion—a right that would be upheld within the state even if *Roe* were to be overturned.[52]

As United Methodists, how are we supposed to respond to these recent bans? Officially, United Methodists still support a woman's right to access abortion, and these bans limit that right. Many of these bans take away a woman's right to consult with a doctor, her sexual partner, and her pastor. The "heartbeat bills" restrict a woman's time of prayerful, thoughtful, and Christian-centered meditation on whether or not an abortion is the best option for her. Instead, she would be rushed to make a hasty decision, one that could increase the mental and spiritual anxiety that all women experience with intended or unintended pregnancies. Many of these bans do not support a woman's right to an abortion in cases of rape or incest, thus revictimizing women who have suffered grave harm at the hands of a stranger, an acquaintance, or a family member. As United Methodists, we affirm continuously the worth and dignity of women and girls around the world. But what kind of affirmation would this be if we ignored those who are victimized and subject them to revictimization by forcing them to carry, birth, and potentially raise a child who is a product of rape or incest? It is crucial that we, as United Methodists, stand against these 2019 abortion bans and continue our support of a woman's right to control her reproductive life, her right to seek counsel in unintended pregnancies, and her right to not be a victim.

---

51 Elizabeth Nash et al., "State Policy Trends at Mid-Year 2019: States Race to Ban or Protect Abortion," Guttmacher Institute, July 1, 2019, https://www.guttmacher .org/article/2019/07/state-policy-trends-mid-year-2019-states-race-ban-or-protect -abortion; Mara Gordon and Alyson Hurt, "Early Abortion Bans: Which States Have Passed Them?" *National Public Radio*, June 5, 2019, https://www.npr.org /sections/health-shots/2019/06/05/729753903/early-abortion-bans-which -states-have-passed-them.

52 Nash et al., "State Policy Trends at Mid-Year 2019: States Race to Ban or Protect Abortion."

Discussion Questions

1. Do you live in a state that has recently limited or expanded abortion rights? How might this action affect women in your local congregation or local community?
2. Does this history help you better understand abortion access as a moral and Christian right?
3. How do you feel about The UMC's current stance on abortion access?
4. How do you feel about their withdrawal from the Religious Coalition for Reproductive Choice?
5. How do you believe your local congregation can do more to help women have access to comprehensive health care?

FIVE: SEXUAL HARASSMENT

When you're serving communion, it's hard for me to concentrate when you say, "This is my body given for you." I think about your body, not Jesus's body.

—Anonymous layman, North Carolina Annual Conference of The United Methodist Church, 2019

We acknowledge that the Church is also a place where sexual misconduct happens when persons in power positions choose to abuse their power. The stories are all too similar. Alleged victims are often reluctant to come forward fearing they will not be believed, or they will experience retaliation and the decision to report will be held against them. Sexual misconduct is a symptom of a systemic problem within our Church and society where patriarchy flourishes.

—Council of Bishops of The United Methodist Church, 2017

By now, most of us have heard of #MeToo, a movement aimed at uncovering and naming the ubiquity of sexual harassment of women. Coined by Tarana Burke in 2006 and amplified by actress Alyssa Milano in 2017, Burke's hashtag wasn't the first of its kind. #WhatWereYouWearing and #YouOkSis existed before #MeToo for a similar reason: to provide a space for victims of domestic violence and sexual assault to have their voices heard. All of these hashtags were begun by women of color. #MeToo became the defining hashtag because it was picked up by a white celebrity who had a high profile and a high following on Twitter. In January 2018, an analysis of Twitter's activity regarding #MeToo "found that the 'virality' of the #MeToo movement was distinct from other discussions about rape and sexual abuse on the Internet." It's been calculated that within a short time span, #MeToo resulted in close to eight million tweets, reaching more than seven million people.[1] #MeToo largely gained traction in Hollywood against the producer Harvey Weinstein and in Washington against white men who hold political power. However, it did bring the conversation beyond Hollywood into the everyday realm of women's secular lives.

Activists, especially millennial and postmillennial activists, today are often criticized for tweeting and not following up with "on the ground" work. However, #MeToo was different. It began a conversation. Many of the tweets were victims' voices, looking to share their stories, without necessarily outing the abuser. This brought a previously not-spoken-of thing that happened to women out in the open. It showed the ubiquity of sexual harassment, assault, and violence that women (and gender-nonconforming people) experience on a daily basis. It showed how prominent and embedded in our culture it is, not only for perpetrators to prey on, harass, and assault women, but for women to not speak of it. Women who are abused in some way are told to simply ignore the abuse or avoid the perpetrator.

But how many people who have heard of #MeToo have also heard of #ChurchToo? In November 2017, a few days after Alyssa Milano's first #MeToo tweet, Emily Joy, a spoken word poet, yoga teacher, and "embodied justice enthusiast," took to Twitter to share her story of abuse. Unlike other #MeToo testimonies, Emily's was set in the church. When she shared her story of abuse at the hands of religious authorities, others joined in and shared theirs. Along with her friend and "co-conspirator" Hannah Paasch, the two decided to create a hashtag to track and unite the stories of church-related or church-centered abuse; thus, #ChurchToo was born. Emily and Hannah recall the hashtag being tweeted thousands of times within the first twenty-four hours. Emily stated, "Victims from all over the country and all over the world were coming forward, detailing harrowing stories of sexual

---

1   Sophie Gilbert, "The Movement of #MeToo: How a Hashtag Got Its Power," October 16, 2017, replicated in "#MeToo Movement: Sexual Hierarchy and Abuse (2016–2018)," chap. 15 in Micah Issitt, *Opinions throughout History: Gender: Roles & Rights* (Amenia, NY: Grey House, 2018).

harassment, assault, and abuse in the church, some of them even naming names. By Wednesday, we were on TIME, Bustle, Vox, Ebony, and a dozen other sites."[2]

When asked what is at the root of church-related and church-centered harassment, abuse, and assault, Emily names multiple things: "patriarchy, male leadership coupled with female submission, purity culture, evangelical personality cult culture, lack of sex-positive and medically accurate sex education, homophobia, and white supremacy."[3] This chapter does not have time to detail or address all of these, but there are other resources out there to begin those conversations if that is your interest.[4]

What this chapter hopes to do, however, is flip the conversation around a bit. #ChurchToo began the conversation about abuse in the church, but it was largely abuse toward female congregants by male clergy or men in leadership. The United Methodist Church has sought to address and eradicate sexual harassment in churches since 1988, when it mandated its first study of the problem. A second study was conducted in 2005 and a third, more recently, in 2017 (just before #MeToo).[5] The UMC has at least addressed clergy abuse of lay members through programs such as Safe Sanctuary and mandatory quadrennial training for all clergy. However, it still fails to hold clergymen fully accountable for their actions—but more on that later.

The church has largely failed to address (until recently) abuse from laypersons toward clergy, specifically the abuse perpetrated by male laypersons toward female clergy. There is no mechanism in place to require laypersons to undergo sexual harassment training. There is no way to excommunicate or punish laypersons who repeatedly harass, abuse, and assault clergywomen within The UMC. And this is the problem. How do you hold laypersons accountable for their actions? Again, this is a question that needs to be asked and answered, but probably not within the confines of these pages. Yet, we can explore the reasons why laypersons, particularly males, feel entitled,

---

2   Emily Joy, "ChurchToo," *Emily Joy Poet* (blog), accessed December 1, 2019, http://emilyjoypoetry.com/churchtoo.

3   Joy.

4   For more on this see Jessica Valenti, *Sex Object: A Memoir* (New York: Dey Street Books, 2017); Nadia Bolz-Weber, *Shameless: A Sexual Reformation* (New York: Convergent Books, 2019); Amy DeRogatis, *Saving Sex: Sexuality and Salvation in American Evangelicalism* (Oxford: Oxford Univ. Press, 2014); and Bromleigh McCleneghan, *Good Christian Sex: Why Chastity Isn't the Only Option and Other Things the Bible Says About Sex* (New York: HarperOne, 2016).

5   These studies have been limited to the United States because, when they began, they were paper surveys, and resources were limited.

justified, and empowered to harass, abuse, and assault clergywomen. Many of the reasons relate to Emily's list, above. Primarily the patriarchal society we live in always empowers males over females, even when females are in positions of authority as leaders of congregations. In this case, gender supersedes professional clout. Nevertheless, female clergy preach.

This chapter is a bit different from the preceding ones. Previous chapters outlined Methodist women's engagement to change political and denominational legislation. This one examines the Methodist side of a conversation that is overtly political and covertly theological. This chapter also uses the word *preach* in direct relation to a woman's voice from the pulpit as it focuses on women clergy. We'll look at stories of female clergy who reported sexual harassment by someone in their congregation; reasons male laypersons feel particularly empowered to commit abuse; and what the reporting process is within Methodism is for such abuse. Therefore, this chapter focuses less on history, because this is such a recent conversation. This chapter's tone will also be a bit different; it speaks in the collective "we" to stress that this is an ongoing conversation necessary for *all* to participate in. It is up to all of us to destigmatize conversations about sexual abuse, at any level and in any place. Women should feel empowered and supported when sharing their stories so that abuse of women makes men feel less powerful.

Why?

Let's begin with *why* abuse happens to women, within or outside of the church. Embedded within most Christian theology is the idea that women are to be submissive and men are to rule over them. This is evident in a variety of overt and covert ways. Prayers are spoken to "Father God." God the Father and God the Son are prioritized over the Holy Spirit, typically translated as a feminine entity. And God is consistently referred to as "He." In art, God is often depicted as a white, bearded male, and Jesus as a white, blond-haired, and blue-eyed man. It's often assumed that men are clergy and women are clergy wives. When women are depicted or discussed, it is often in the role of mother—compassionate, caring, submissive, sexless. Covertly, when we read scripture, we typically focus on the male characters: Jesus, the disciples, Paul, Moses. We prioritize the writings and testimonies of males: Matthew, Mark, Luke, John, Paul. We rarely speak about women in scripture on a weekly basis, and if we do it's only in their relationship to men: Mary, mother of Jesus; Mary Magdalene, the prostitute (who wasn't actually a prostitute but was mislabeled to discredit her) whom Jesus was kind enough to forgive; or the unnamed "woman at the well" and "the hemorrhaging woman." Yes, these were all written during a highly patriarchal time, and we cannot create an entirely new canon that includes the voices and writings of women who were also disciples and apostles of Jesus and whose writings were ignored in the first few centuries of Christian interpretation and canonization, but we can reexamine scripture in order to highlight the stories of women for what they are: stories of women. We can look at stories through their lens, honor their voices, their experience.

But on a weekly basis, we don't. Why? Because we don't want to shake up a congregation. If you're a woman, you don't want to come off as the angry feminist preacher who can't help herself. You don't want to risk being moved to another congregation because you caused too much trouble in your current one. You also don't want to be "the woman preacher" who only preaches about women. (Note: there are *some* amazing, brave, and ministry-changing women and gender-nonconforming people who do this work weekly and do it well.) If you're a male clergyperson, you either don't because you don't want to pretend to speak for women or know women's experience, or it could be that you just don't give a damn enough to even try. And this is the problem that perpetuates Christian patriarchy. (Note: this is not an exhaustive list of the ways and reasons that Christian patriarchy is perpetuated. There are many other reasons that dozens of books have detailed.) This is what empowers male laypersons to feel that they are somehow closer to God, more empowered by God, because they believe that the male body more accurately reflects the image of God. This is what allows men to feel that they have authority over a clergywoman because she is a woman first, a clergy member second.

Women can experience sexual harassment or assault literally anywhere they go. Gender and society's sexism unfortunately are rampant and rather universal. In fact, a 2020 United Nations report states that 90 percent of the world's population is biased against women in some way.[6] Within the church, however, there seems to be a heightened experience of harassment and assault for women who lead. Why? It has to do with the message that Christian theologians and preachers have consistently preached for now over two millennia—the submissiveness of women. Women who, in the church setting, defy this message directly by daring to follow a call to ministry and

---

6 Pedro Conceição et al., "Tackling Social Norms: A Game Changer for Gender Inequalities" (New York: United Nations Development Programme, 2020), http:// hdr.undp.org/sites/default/files/hd_perspectives_gsni.pdf. See also, Liz Ford, "Nine out of 10 people found to be biased against women," *Guardian* (UK), March 5, 2020, https://www.theguardian.com/global-development/2020/mar/05/nine-out -of-10-people-found-to-be-biased-against-women

lead a congregation are targeted more than other women in a congregation for their overt challenge to what many believe to be "Christian tradition" and "scriptural authority."

The Stained-Glass Ceiling

The stained-glass ceiling is a metaphor, similar to the glass ceiling that women experience in the secular world. The glass ceiling is a metaphor for how women can see opportunities ahead of them but are prevented from breaking through due to hegemonic femininity and systemic misogyny and sexism, all of which assume women cannot and should not be leaders in the world. Author Ann Morrison describes the problem in the corporate world as a ceiling that is "so subtle that it is transparent, yet so strong that it prevents women from moving up the corporate hierarchy."[7] The same problem exists in the church. Women see the levels of upward mobility as clergy but are prevented from attaining them simply because they are women seeking to assert themselves in a patriarchal institution.

In her book, *Under the Stained Glass Ceiling*, Rev. Dr. Beth Cooper argues that "ignorance, shame, and culturally accepted gender inequities stand behind the problems that persist in the church."[8] This stained-glass ceiling prevents women from fully being able to thrive professionally—and spiritually—within the church, keeping them in smaller congregations, where they earn less pay and less respect. Dr. Cooper's work also outlines the sexual harassment of United Methodist (UM) clergywomen. Her research began in 1997, when she interviewed clergywomen who had been harassed while serving in UM congregations. In 2003, she conducted a more formal survey, the Survey of Clergywomen and Sexual Harassment in The United Methodist Church, the first of its kind. The results of the study were so shocking that they needed to be confirmed by the Commission on the Status and Role of Women (COSROW), a general agency within The UMC tasked with monitoring and supporting women in the denomination. Dr. Cooper's findings were substantiated. COSROW's 2005 survey found that "three quarters of clergywomen and half of laywomen have been sexually harassed in the local church."[9]

---

7   Ann Morrison, *Breaking the Glass Ceiling: Can Women Reach the Top of America's Largest Corporations?* (n.p.: Perseus, 1987).

8   Beth Cooper, *Under the Stained Glass Ceiling: Sexual Harassment of United Methodist Clergywomen* (San Diego: Frontrowliving Press, 2011), 11.

9   Cooper, 12.

Dr. Cooper's findings include the following trends: (1) All women experienced sexual harassment no matter their age, class, race, or marital status. (2) Despite the policies that have been adapted and implemented at the denominational level, still over half of clergywomen had experienced harassment while serving. (3) It cannot be up to clergywomen alone to implement policies and procedures; they need additional support from church leaders and members. (4) Names are often used as a way to denigrate women based on their gender, even if these names tend to refer more to sexual orientation: *lesbian*, *dyke*, *whore*, and *bitch*. These words are meant to put women down based on their gender alone and have nothing to do with sexual orientation when they're used. (5) Clergywomen are harassed more often by laity than by other clergy or church leaders (arguably because these clergy are required to undergo sexual harassment training).[10]

The church creates a unique setting for sexual harassment due to the separation of church and state. Rights to privacy and against improper, invasive, and overly personal questions from which women have protection in the secular workplace do not apply to the church when seeking employment. Denominations are allowed to not hire women because they are women. Two of the largest factions of the Christian faith—the Roman Catholic Church and the Southern Baptist Convention—prevent the ordination of and preaching of women based on gender alone. In any other field this would be sex discrimination, but the church is not required to follow the same hiring procedures as other institutions. In the same light, parish hiring committees or ordination committees are allowed to ask women overtly personal and intimate questions about their sexual and marital lives, questions that would raise a red flag in any other profession. Everything is put on the table when it comes to following a call to ministry, and there are virtually no rights protecting women from these types of questions, verbal harassments, and invasions of privacy. To understand the persistent problem of sexual harassment of clergywomen, this chapter relies on stories told by clergywomen. They are taken from a variety of sources: published surveys from COSROW, Dr. Cooper's recorded testimonies in *Under the Stained Glass Ceiling*, Twitter, and blogs.

The United Methodist Church has a rather stringent ordination process where candidates for ministry are asked to do multiple interviews with various committees. Questions pertain to theological training, faith development, leadership experience, and personal morality. During this process, their lives are laid out on the table. No question is off-limits. Women—and men—are

---

10 Cooper, 18.

asked about how they understand God, how they interpret scripture, their leadership style, their love life, their friendships, their family history, their sexual history, their medical history. Everything about them is laid before a committee of strangers to determine if they are worthy moral examples. Dr. Cooper records some of these stories in her book. One read, "A second career woman sought ordination in her annual conference. Recently divorced, the details of the divorce were not the business of the interview. The interviewing committee asked her if her desire to pursue ordained ministry was the reason behind her divorce."[11] In no other profession should one's marital life have anything to do with the interview process or being qualified for a job. Inquiring why one is divorced and suggesting that it is related to a call to ministry is abhorrent. The harassment around divorce doesn't end with the candidacy and interview process. When a congregation finds out that a clergywoman has been divorced, they often criticize and blame her. For one victim, congregants critiqued her ministry by saying, "If she couldn't hold her marriage together, how would she ever be successful at [holding our] church [together]?"[12] In any other occupation, there is a process for filing complaints when subjected to comments and questions like this. But not in the ministry. Instead, it's par for the course; it's expected. The reasoning behind this is that if you are going to be the moral leader of a congregation, then you must exemplify a moral life—and apparently this necessitates having a happy and stable marriage.

Single women also face harassment for their marital status. They are more often placed in churches in small towns, where their lives become the gossip of the town. If they dare to venture to the nearest city for a girls' night or even a date, the agenda of the night becomes the next day's gossip. People wonder who she went with, why she was out so late, if she drank, if she brought someone home with her. Dr. Cooper states that single clergywomen "live in a fish bowl," and they are treated with no more respect than "a teenager in their family." Single clergywomen reported to Dr. Cooper that "it was hard to have a life outside the church because of social presumptions" and "no friendship is safe from presumptions." If a single clergywoman befriended a man, she was seen as "loose," and if she befriended a woman, there were rumors that she was a lesbian.[13]

Single clergywomen are in an entirely different category from married clergywomen because within American society, even today, it is presumed

---

11 Cooper, 23.
12 Cooper, 25.
13 Cooper, 25.

that if a woman reaches a certain age and is still single, then something must be wrong with her. The list of potential reasons something is supposedly wrong with a single woman illustrate the double standard to which women are subjected. Maybe she's too bossy, too needy. Maybe she's too loose or too uptight. Maybe she doesn't care for herself enough, or maybe she's too high-maintenance. Perhaps she speaks her mind too often, or maybe she's too shy. Single women's lives are open to criticism and justified as being criticized because their marital status presumes that they are living outside of the norm.

Women's physical appearance was consistently judged as well. From weight to dress to hairstyle and makeup, the way clergywomen present themselves is a constant reminder of one thing—sex. Laymen often reported to their clergywomen that they couldn't help but see them as sexual beings, and in each case, somehow this was the clergywoman's fault for being a woman. How dare she? One woman reported to Dr. Cooper that she once preached without her robe while wearing a dress that showed her knees. After the service, a layman approached her and said he couldn't concentrate the entire service because of *his* sexual feelings.[14] Another woman was pregnant and was asked to wear a larger robe that didn't show her pregnant belly because her belly reminded her congregants that she was sexual. Even when women conform to social standards (i.e., motherhood), they are asked to cover themselves, for the only thing that comes to mind is, *Our clergywoman has had sex!* This request would never be asked of a male clergy who was an expectant father. Another woman, who was overweight, remembered how embarrassed she was when her district committee on ordained ministry commented on her weight and suggested that this might keep her from being ordained.[15]

Women were also judged for wearing makeup, and for not wearing makeup. If a woman chose to not wear makeup to challenge the conventional beauty standards that women are expected to maintain, their congregants abhorred them—in one case, even to the point where the clergywoman was approached by the staff parish relations committee and told that she must start wearing makeup because she is a professional.[16] Somehow professional stature is tied to standards of beauty. Another woman reported that her love of makeup and of treating herself to spas was deemed inappropriate. Her staff parish relations committee informed her that she was not

---

14 Cooper, 26.
15 Cooper, 23.
16 Cooper, 26.

being professional and was beginning to look like a "slut" for wearing too much "red lipstick." Other members of her congregation said they couldn't believe she would spend so much money on stuff like that. This woman was, justifiably, astounded and told Dr. Cooper, "Not only did they presume to tell me what I could and could not do at work, but also how I was to spend my money, and what I was to look like at work."[17]

These standards are not new. Remember Rev. Anna Howard Shaw, ordained clergywoman, president of NAWSA, and suffragist from chapter 1? Here's her story. Always quick on her feet, Shaw knew how to captivate an audience and break down the arguments of her male opponents. She was rarely intimidated by their status, prowess, or gender. She was also not distracted by comments on her personal appearance. While giving a lecture in Chautauqua, a local male minister "deplored [her] fashion" for "wearing [her] hair short." He asked her why she continued to wear her hair short, as this went against what most "respectable" women did. He went so far as to guess that she "had been ill and that [her] hair has fallen out." Shaw responded in her typical manner, "I will admit frankly that it is a birth mark. I was born with short hair."[18] Unafraid to counter the sexist arguments of another male minister, Shaw refuted his critique with charming wit. She later stated, however, that the minster was right to inquire about her hair: "A few years later I let my hair grow long, for I had learned that no woman in public life can afford to make herself conspicuous by any eccentricity of dress or appearance. If she does so she suffers for it herself, which may not disturb her, and to a greater or less degree she injures the cause she represents, which should disturb her very much."[19] Shaw knew 150 years ago that women who wanted to be in the public eye had to conform to certain standards while seeking to undo other standards that are imposed on them. This rhetoric has not gone away. Even today, women are expected to maintain a certain standard of beauty in order to be taken seriously. For Shaw this was difficult. She was unlike other suffragists of her time. She was an immigrant, raised in poverty, and pushed to the brink of starvation during her education. She did not get involved with the women's movement as a way to spend her white, middle-class leisure time. For Shaw and other clergywomen, the ministry is a calling, not a hobby. Nevertheless, they preached.

---

17 Cooper, 27.

18 Anna Howard Shaw, "The Widening Suffrage Stream," chap. 11 in *The Story of a Pioneer*, http://www.gutenberg.org/files/354/354-h/354-h.htm#link2H_4_0009.

19 Shaw, chap. 11.

Dr. Cooper has recorded dozens of stories like these throughout her book. These stories dictate how entitled laypersons feel to judge and harass clergywomen because they are women who do not conform to the standards that society has set for them or the standards they believe the church has set for them. Dr. Cooper noted more serious allegations as well, of rape, stalking, and physical abuse—all of which were perpetrated against clergywomen by male members of their congregations. These men felt entitled to dominate their female clergy because they deemed that the women had somehow stepped out of their place by following a call.

More recently, in June 2019, the North Carolina Annual Conference's Commission on the Status and Role of Women debuted a video at its annual conference session that invited male clergy to read aloud quotes that laymen had said to female clergy. The video immediately went viral in the Methodist virtual world and sparked discussion among US clergypersons about sexual harassment of clergywomen. It gave much-needed attention to the fact that sometimes it is clergy who are harassed by congregants, particularly when the clergy are women.

Some of the statements discussed clergywomen's bodies:

"I can't concentrate on your sermon because you're so pretty."

"Women shouldn't wear pants."

"Well, you don't pray as well as the former pastor, but you sure are prettier."

"I keep picturing you naked under your robe."

"When you're serving communion, it's hard for me to concentrate when you say, This is my body, given for you.' I think about your body, not Jesus's body."

"I usually don't say this to a minister, but you're really cute."[20]

Others questioned their authority or ability to preach:

"You're going to hell, you know[.] God doesn't permit women to preach. It's in the Bible."

"When you walked in for the introductory visit, we thought you were the pastor's wife, and we kept looking for the pastor."

"If more men would step up and do what God was calling them to do, we wouldn't need the weaker sex to preach."

---

20 NC Conference of The UMC, "Women in Ministry," June 2019, https://vimeo.com/335862568.

"I've never met one of you. Is this something you felt God calling you to do or something that you just wanted to do [*wink*]?"

"You do a good job, but I think scripture is more meaningful when read with a male voice."

"This is a big job for *you*."[21]

The male ministers reading the statements fumbled their way through them, mostly in shock that these things had actually been said directly to fellow clergywomen. Most women who watched the video nodded in solidarity. They had heard eerily similar and appalling things throughout their careers and their calls. Again, the video went viral, sometimes accompanied by the #ChurchToo hashtag, indicating that abuse happens in the church and clarifying that it isn't always clergymen who are the abusers.

Data on the Stained-Glass Ceiling

The stained-glass ceiling is in full effect. It is the "unspoken cap that limits [women's] ministries."[22] It's the notion that when women feel unsafe in a congregation, they are moved to another congregation. If they dare to speak up and report the incident, their careers are stained. Dr. Cooper reported that some clergywomen who were ordained at the same time as clergymen were often paid less, were given smaller churches, and were more often assigned as assistant pastors than as senior pastors. An article in the *New York Times* confirmed this phenomenon beyond UM churches: "In their second decade in ordained ministry, however, 70 percent of men had moved on to medium-sized congregations . . . By comparison, only 37 percent of women led medium and large congregations."[23] The stained-glass ceiling isn't a problem only within The UMC. Paul Sullins, professor at Catholic University of America, wrote "The Stained Glass Ceiling: Career Attainment for Women Clergy," an article detailing how rampant this problem is among other mainline Protestant denominations. His article compares the success rate of women clergy in the Episcopal Church (EC) and the Presbyterian Church in the United States of America (PCUSA). His findings confirm that clergywomen "are over-represented in subordinate positions and those

---

21 NC Conference.
22 Cooper, *Under the Stained Glass Ceiling,* 32.
23 As quoted in Cooper, 32.

having lower status," a status that seems to remain constant over the career of a clergywoman.[24]

However, this subordinate, lower-class status only pertains to women who remain in the parish field; those who move up the administrative ranks tend to have a higher status, and these ranks tend to have less gender disparity than the parish ministry. Sullins uses arguments made in the 1980s and '90s by Mark Chaves, Frederick Schmidt, and Edward C. Lehman, who all theorize that women were kept in lower-status positions of parish ministry when compared to their male colleagues.[25] In other words, gender disparity tends to happen most at the congregational level. Women are kept in smaller churches and as assistant pastors to a male senior pastor. Once a woman's call moves beyond the parish to the bureaucratic levels of the denomination, gender disparity evens out. Women and men have a closer percentage when it comes to being bishops and/or working in a general agency. So the problem doesn't lie with the bureaucracy, necessarily, but with the theological understandings of the local church.

Sullins sought to update this analysis and focus on an in-depth analysis of the EC and see whether or not his data was substantiated when compared to the PCUSA. His main question was, "Is the lower job attainment of women a product of the newness of women's entry into a formerly all-male domain, or does it reflect more persistent structural disparity regarding women?" He also asked whether the gender disparity was "diminishing or continuing in full force." Sullins found that the lower job attainment of women was more of a systemic issue. Bishops in the EC largely supported women in ministry, but in the parish women were more likely to be given a smaller parish or be placed as an assistant pastor (with a male as senior pastor).[26]

Denominations like being known for ordaining women; it makes them look progressive. However, ordained women are not treated equally to their male counterparts after ordination. Men are given the bigger pulpits at a faster pace and are more likely to be named as senior pastor, for "ordination is one thing, deployment is another."[27] At the institutional level, denomina-

---

24 Paul Sullins, "The Stained Glass Ceiling: Career Attainment for Women Clergy," *Sociology of Religion* 61, no. 3 (Autumn 2000): 243.

25 Mark Chaves, *Ordaining Women: Culture and Conflict in Religious Organizations* (Cambridge, MA: Harvard Univ. Press, 1997); Frederick Schmidt, *A Still Small Voice: Women, Ordination, and the Church* (Syracuse, NY: Syracuse Univ. Press 1996); and Edward C. Lehman, "Patterns of Lay Resistance to Women in Ministry," *Sociological Analysis* 41, no. 4 (Winter 1980): 317–38.

26 Sullins, "Stained Glass Ceiling," 244.

27 Schmidt, *A Still Small Voice*, 26, quoted in Sullins, 244.

tions can approve the ordination of women rather quickly, and this change can be implemented within a few years. However, it takes the culture of the church, the people who sit in the pews, longer to accept the authority and ordination of a woman—this is the heart of the stained-glass ceiling. Sullins found that in the twenty years that the EC has ordained women, there has been no change in the resistance to women as religious authority figures; thus, this is a systemic problem. He argues, "It appears that male/female inequality among the clergy is not due to formal institutional discrimination but is a result of embedded cultural values, values that are particularly resident in congregations and that show no indication of changing."[28] Despite women's gains in the secular world (even though there is still a long way to go to achieve full equity), in the clerical world, women seem to have not gained nearly as much.

Sullins conducted his research in 1999 and published in 2000. Since then several other studies have confirmed his findings. In 2015, a National Congregations Study report found that there is "essentially no overall increase in the number of congregations led by women since 1998, with about 11 percent of congregations being led by women."[29] This study was directed by Mark Chaves (whose theoretical work was used by Sullins) at Duke University and is the third of its kind. It examines religion at large, focusing on Christian denominations but inclusive of non-Christian experience as well. Chaves declares, "The 'stained-glass ceiling' is real." The data from the survey is available online in an interactive format. If you look at the data by gender, some of the disparities come to life. When asked, "Can women be religious leaders?" 57.7 percent said yes, 41.6 percent said no, and 0.7 percent didn't know. This question was then analyzed by political ideology (with 86.4 percent of liberals saying yes, 46.7 percent of conservatives saying yes), by region (with the Northeast giving the most approval and the South giving the least), by religious tradition (with white liberals or moderates giving the most approval and Roman Catholics giving the most disapproval), and by theological leanings (with liberal theologies approving 90 percent and conservative theologies disapproving by 51.7 percent).

---

28 Sullins, 261.

29 Eric Ferreri, "Study: Female Church Leaders Face Stained-Glass Ceiling," December 9, 2015. The data collected from the study can be found at http://www.soc.duke.edu/natcong/explore.html. An analysis of the study can be found in Mark Chaves and Shawna L. Anderson, "Changing American Congregations: Findings from the Third Wave of the National Congregations Study," *Journal for the Scientific Study of Religion* 53: 676–86, available online at http://www.soc.duke.edu/natcong/Docs/Changing_American_Congs.pdf.

When analyzed by size of congregation, 68 percent of those with fewer than 50 members agreed that women could be leaders. As the congregation size increased, the approval rating decreased. In congregations with more than 1,000 members, 21.9 percent said women could be religious leaders and 78.1 percent said they could not.[30] This confirms what was previously stated by Sullins—women are more likely to serve smaller congregations. Thus, this 2015 study infers that smaller congregations have more than likely had women serving as their leaders and are, therefore, more likely to accept their authority as a religious leader. Similar responses were given to the question, "Can women preach?"[31]

When asked about the gender of the religious leader, 88.6 percent of congregations reported a male and 11.4 percent reported a female. Again the data supports Sullins's findings. When it comes to the size of congregation, women are more likely to serve parishes with fewer than 100 members (50 or less, 13.9 percent female; 51–100 members, 14 percent; 101–250 members, 7.8 percent; 251–1,000 members, 4.6 percent; more than 1,000 members, 3.4 percent). As the membership increases, the likelihood of having a female clergyperson decreases.[32] The stained-glass ceiling is, indeed, real and ongoing.

The United Methodist Church follows the trends of these surveys; however, the denomination has a higher percentage of female clergy. The UMC was one of the first mainline Protestant denominations to ordain women (1956); thus, women have been serving congregations longer. So, while the trends are similar, the percentage of women serving is actually higher in The UMC than the national average of 11 percent. COSROW reports that as of 2019, women make up 31.2 percent of clergy, 38.5 percent of UMC agency heads, and 27.3 percent of bishops.[33] A more comprehensive 2014 survey conducted by COSROW broke down the numbers by type of clergy. Women make up 29 percent of elders in full connection, 72 percent of deacons in full connection, 28 percent of full-time local pastors, 32 percent of part-time local pastors, and 41 percent of provisional elders.[34] One of the more telling

30 The Association of Religion Data Archives, "Can Women Be Religious Leaders?" accessed February 20, 2020, http://www.thearda.com/ConQS/qs_250.asp.

31 The Association of Religion Data Archives, "Can Women Preach?" February 20, 2020, http://www.thearda.com/ConQS/qs_249.asp.

32 The Association of Religion Data Archives, "Gender of Religious Leader," accessed February 20, 2020, http://www.thearda.com/ConQS/qs_236.asp.

33 General Commission on the Status and Role of Women (hereinafter GCOSROW), "Gender in the UMC," 2019.

34 GCOSROW, "Women by the Numbers," 2014.

pieces from these statistics is the drop between women who are provisional elders and women who are elders in full connection. Provisional status is a residency status given to candidates and is the final stepping-stone in the ordination process. What this shows is that women experience something during their provisional years that prevents them from either seeking to become or actually becoming elders in full connection. There is no data to support what happens, but one could infer that during their provisional membership, women see their authority questioned based on their gender or they experience some of sort of sexual misconduct that turns them away from the ministry. When looking at ongoing trends, "the numbers of clergywomen who are elders in full connection is not increasing at a steady rate as in years past."[35]

How does this relate to the harassment of clergywomen? Clergywomen experience sexual harassment at any level of the church, no matter the parish size. However, given that women are more likely to be the senior pastors of smaller churches, sexual harassment occurs more at this level. In 2017, CGOSROW conducted a survey of sexual misconduct within The UMC and received 4,374 responses. They found that between 1990 and 2005 reports of sexual misconduct rose, but between 2005 and 2017 they decreased in all areas of ministry except seminaries. It also found that women experience more sexual misconduct than men and that "clergy are more at risk to experience all behaviors than laity." Nearly 70 percent of clergy reported experiencing sexual misconduct.[36] The most common type of sexual misconduct for women was sexist comments/jokes (47.7 percent), followed by suggestive looks/leers (44.6 percent) and touching/closeness (44.3 percent).[37] Most often, the perpetrators were reported to be local church members, 52.5 percent. Thus, this 2017 study confirms that Dr. Cooper's argument that male lay members are more likely to harass female clergywomen. GCOSROW's analysis confirms this:

> Interestingly, the most common perpetrator in each setting is not a person of great power, at least as traditionally defined. Certainly, in the workplace and school, colleagues and fellow students are not more powerful than others in those locations, but the local church is different. A member COULD be powerful, if a long-time member or a generous giver, for example. Like clients in a workplace, it is difficult to tell a "customer" that

---

35 GCOSROW, "Women by the Numbers."
36 GCOSROW, "Sexual Misconduct in The United Methodist Church: US Update," Summer 2017, 4.
37 GCOSROW, 5.

they have sexually harassed you, for fear they will leave and take their business elsewhere.[38]

While in the church setting, people tend to think of the clergy as the authority, but ask any clergyperson and they will agree that there are certain laypersons who wield an exceptional amount of influential authority. Whether this authority is through donations or legacy, certain lay members feel empowered to direct how and what the local parish does. If a clergyperson is new and wants to change certain things about how the church looks, how it functions, or who it does ministry with, those empowered laypersons are most likely to showcase their disagreement in some fashion. If the clergyperson happens to be a woman, one of the ways to show power is through demeaning comments based on gender, assertive touching, rumors, threat of physical assault, or actual physical assault.

The most common response to assault from a layperson was avoiding the perpetrator (50.8 percent) or ignoring the incident (46.3 percent).[39] Of those who had the courage to report the behavior, 52.9 percent felt that they were "believed, supported, and corrective action was taken," and a close 40.3 percent said that "the complaint was minimized, trivialized, or dismissed."[40] This statistic is too close for comfort. In order for women to feel comfortable reporting abuse when it happens, they need to know that, no matter who the perpetrator is, they will be supported and corrective action will be taken. Too often this is not the case. Women are frequently blamed and even punished. In the parish setting, such punishment most often comes in the form of moving the female clergy to a different congregation. Thus, even if women have the courage to report abuse, the problem is "solved" through avoidance and ignorance.

GCOSROW and other general agencies of The UMC have worked to end or at least lessen sexual misconduct within The UMC. Through resolutions, education, training, and church policies, they have sought to implement accountability at all levels. The United Methodist Church does have a reporting process in place. Clergy are asked to report all allegations of sexual harassment, assault, or abuse to their district superintendent and/or bishop. Sometimes this happens. Sometimes, however, women believe that their careers will be harmed for reporting these instances, so they choose to avoid and/or ignore the perpetuator. Many times the incidents aren't reported. Women are fearful that they won't be believed and that instead

38 GCOSROW, 7.
39 GCOSROW, 7.
40 GCOSROW, 8.

of the abuser being called out, they themselves will be moved to another congregation. The problem is that when or if charges are brought against a layperson, they are usually resolved by the district superintendent (if brought by the clergy) or by the clergy (if brought by another lay member). Most Methodist historians will agree a complaint against a layperson has never made it all the way to a church trial, the only place where a layperson could truly be punished or held accountable for their actions.

The harassment of clergywomen also rarely makes news. More often than not, stories are buried to maintain either the power or status of the abuser or the reputation of the denomination, congregation, or pastor. I was only able to find one article in recent history that detailed a mishandling of a sexual harassment complaint against a layperson. In 2017 a sexual misconduct case in the North Texas Annual Conference made denominational news. The Reverend Yvette Blair-Lavallais, a black clergywoman, was sexually harassed by a white male layperson while serving as an associate pastor. According to Reverend Blair-Lavallais, "the man repeatedly touched her inappropriately despite her protests and rebuffs."[41] She reported the harassment to her senior pastor, Rev. Andy Lewis, a white man, who did nothing. The harassment continued. When Reverend Blair-Lavallais learned that she was not the perpetrator's only victim, she went to the police. But the police found no evidence. As a result of this process, Reverend Blair-Lavallais was moved to another church. Soon after, it was announced that Reverend Lewis, the senior pastor who had ignored her complaints, was promoted by the bishop of North Texas to a higher position within the conference office. Reverend Blair-Lavallais filed a complaint against Reverend Lewis to contest his promotion.[42] What is interesting here is that the official complaint process was followed. However, the complaint was filed against the other clergy member for ignoring the original abuse, and not the abuser himself. It's as if Reverend Blair-Lavallais knew it was pointless to try to file an official complaint against a layperson because there are virtually no repercussions. No one will take a complaint seriously enough to remove a layperson from membership.

However, someone might listen to a complaint against a fellow clergyperson for ignoring a sexual harassment complaint. But that didn't happen either. Despite repeated attempts by allies of Reverend Blair-Lavallais

41 United Methodist Insight, "What Do We Really Need to Know? Clergywoman's Complaint Finds Gaps between Process and Justice," June 8, 2017, https://um-insight .net/in-the-church/ordained-ministry/what-do-we-really-need-to-know/.
42 United Methodist Insight.

to discuss sexual harassment of clergywomen as a systemic problem at the 2017 Annual Conference Session of North Texas, the bishop dismissed requests and cited "the process." In other words, talking openly about how and why clergywomen are sexually harassed by laymen and why their complaints are not taken seriously by those who are in a position to help was not a matter for public discussion; it was to be handled privately, through the proper process.[43] Many annual conferences, including North Texas, claim to have zero-tolerance policies when it comes to sexual harassment. However, when it comes to clergywomen filing complaints against laymen, zero tolerance does not apply to the victim. Instead, the victim is punished by being ignored, revictimized, and relocated. Even the policies The UMC has in place do not work to protect all victims; thus, new solutions, new policies, and more open conversations are needed. Nevertheless, despite being harassed, being ignored, and being revictimized by the denomination she served, Reverend Blair-Lavallais continued to preach.

The need to bring attention to the harassment of clergywomen by laymen, however, does not mean we can ignore or have somehow solved the problem of clergymen harassing laywomen. That is not the intention of this chapter. In fact, while research for this book was in process, a case made national headlines in the West Ohio Annual Conference. Four women accused Rev. Donald "Bud" Heckman of sexual misconduct and abuse. It is the first sexual misconduct complaint to become public knowledge since the rise in popularity of #MeToo in 2017.[44] With the threat of facing a church trial, the complaint was resolved through a resolution process, in which the four abused women were not allowed to take part. Reverend Heckman agreed to early retirement and publicly acknowledged "his personal regret" for the sexual misconduct. However, he is allowed to retain his clergy credentials and continue to call himself a minister.[45] This resolution was reached on January 2, 2020, one day after punitive measures went into effect stating that any United Methodist minister who performed multiple same-sex weddings would immediately lose their license. It is evidence of how far The United Methodist Church must come in order to take sexual misconducts accusations, resolutions, and punishments seriously. These four women, and the

---

43 United Methodist Insight.

44 Heather Hahn, "Clergyman Accused of Sexual Misconduct, Abuse," United Methodist News Service, October 17, 2019, https://www.umnews.org/en/news/clergyman -accused-of-sexual-misconduct-abuse.

45 Heather Hahn, "Clergyman Retires 'Under Complaint' of Abuse," United Methodist News Service, January 2, 2020, https://www.umnews.org/en/news/clergyman -retires-under-complaint-of-abuse.

countless others who have not come forward or whose complaints never made national headlines, deserve to see more justice than this resolution afforded them.

The bulk of the #MeToo and #ChurchToo movements rarely call out individuals by name for their harassment, assault, or abuse. Instead, the movements are concerned with calling out the culture, or in the case of #ChurchToo, the theology that allows the disparaging of women to continue to take place and be accepted. The same goes for clergywomen who experienced harassment, assault, or abuse. There is rarely an advantage in naming the perpetrator because there is seldom accountability or punishment for the crime. One solution the church should seek is addressing the theological inconsistencies that create harassment in the first place. COSROW has begun to produce resources for this exact purpose, among them, *Women Called to Ministry*, which examines women of the Bible, named and unnamed, their ministries, and the ministries that they inspire. It guides women who are feeling a call to ministry and supports them in that endeavor. It also helps others understand how and why women are called to ministry and how and why that call should be understood as legitimate.[46] Another is "God of the Bible," which helps churches understand how and why to use more expansive language when referencing God. It "challenges participants to strengthen their personal relationship with God by removing barriers of human limitations from our understanding of who God is."[47] In other words, when we remove the human limitation of God being a white male, what type of God might we encounter? What new relationship with God might we have? Other resources that they've recently produced are outlined the concluding chapter.

This final chapter highlights the continuous problem with religion in general, Christianity specifically: an unwillingness to see women as fully made in the image of God and therefore worthy of equal respect before the law and within social locations, worthy of full bodily rights, worthy of authority, and worthy of being heard. Despite data and testimony, The UMC endorses gender equity in its own *Book of Discipline*. Paragraph 161 of the Social

46 Delia Halverson et al., *Women Called to Ministry: A Six-Session Study for The United Methodist Church: Leader's Study Guide* (GCOSROW, 2015), https://www.gcsrw.org/Portals/13/Women-Called-to-Ministry/English-Leader.pdf. A similar resource is "Words That Hurt, Words That Heal," produced alongside United Methodist Women in 2013.

47 Rev. Aida Fernandez, Dr. Susan Hylen, and Rev. Adrienne Trevathan, *God of the Bible: A Study for United Methodists about How God Is Revealed in Scripture: Leader's Study Guide* (GCOSROW, 2017), https://www.gcsrw.org/Portals/13/God-of-the-Bible/God-of-the-Bible-Book-Leader's-Guide-2017.pdf.

Principles states, "We reject the erroneous notion that one gender is superior to another."[48] It further states the consequences of believing one to be superior to another: "Sexual harassment must be understood as an exploitation of a power relationship."[49] These are necessary statements for a denomination to make in an official capacity. However, how many clergy know what the current *Book of Discipline* says? How many laypersons know what the *Book of Discipline* is? For these statements (and other statements made by The UMC in any official capacity) to have any positive effect, there must be action. Someone must take the words from the page and preach them from the pulpit. Someone must teach gender equity in Sunday schools and Bible studies. Someone must exegete using feminist, queer, and womanist interpretations, which promote an alternative reading of scripture. These things must happen in order for the denomination to move beyond an endorsement of gender equity to a living out of gender equity.

For two thousand years, the majority of Christians believed that women are not made in the image of the God the same way that men are. And some taught that women do not even have souls. These beliefs prevented women from having access to the pulpit and to having any sense of religious authority. It was this same idea that prevented women from, supposedly, having the full intellectual capability to vote. It's the same rationale that prevented women from being recognized as equal before the law or as worthy of making their own decisions regarding their reproductive lives. It's the same rationale that gives male clergy the gall to sexually harass their female congregants, and male congregants to make inappropriate comments about their female clergy.

Until we can admit that women are, in fact, created as equals in the image of God, we will have to deal with misogynistic theology that assumes they are lesser. How do we do this? Any basic gender-theory class will tell you that gender is a performance based in scripts that are handed down generation by generation, culture by culture, that tell women how they are to act if they want to be worthy of the title of woman. The same can be said of religion. It, too, is a performance full of scripts that are handed down from one generation to the next. We have to start with changing the scripts. This is as easy as using gender-neutral pronouns to refer to God and correcting those who continuously refer to God as He; highlighting the stories of women in the Bible through their own viewpoints; and reading or employing

---

48 *Book of Discipline of The United Methodist Church* (Nashville: United Methodist Publishing House, 2016), ¶161f.
49 *Book of Discipline*, 2016, ¶161j.

a work of feminist, womanist, or queer theology to exegete a familiar text. Scripts can be changed. Christian culture and theology can be changed in order to fully understand women as equally made in the image of God. We just have to be intentional when we speak and not be afraid to name women as fully equal until their equality becomes the script.

Discussion Questions

1. If your congregation has a female clergyperson, how do you all support her in her ministry?
2. How can your support improve, given what you've read in this chapter?
3. Which resource from COSROW might your local congregation use to help change the scripts we use when talking about gender and God in the church?
4. Has your pastor preached using a feminist, queer, or womanist lens? Would you like to hear a sermon preached using such a lens? Why? Why not?
5. What can your congregation do to discuss the #MeToo and #ChurchToo movements from the lens of Christian faith?

CONCLUSION: SHE CONTINUES TO PREACH

> This is a book about women—women in the churches, but other women
> as well, for there is no clear dividing line. The women's movement is the
> newest among the many of our time. Yet in another sense it is not new,
> for its occasional manifestations and the conditions which produce them
> go back to the beginnings of human history.
> —Georgia Harkness, *Women in Church and Society*

In the fall of 2019, another social media campaign was launched to support clergywomen. #NotGoingHome went viral after Pastor John MacArthur disparaged Beth Moore, a woman and prominent Southern Baptist speaker. MacArthur was contributing to the ongoing debate within the Southern Baptist Convention (SBC) on whether or not women should be allowed to preach. He claimed that by letting Beth Moore come close to preaching, the SBC has "given up biblical authority" by taking a "headlong plunge" toward the ordination of women.[1] Asked to give his two-word response to the idea of "Beth Moore," MacArthur doubled down and said, "Go home."

---

1   Bob Smietana, "Accusing SBC of 'Caving,' John MacArthur Says of Beth Moore: 'Go Home,'" *Religion News*, October 19, 2019, https://religionnews.com/2019/10/19/accusing-sbc-of-caving-john-macarthur-says-beth-moore-should-go-home/.

His response immediately led to a Twitter and social media campaign largely run by women pastors who used the hashtag #NotGoingHome to show that their proper place is in the pulpit, not in the home. Videos of women preaching were posted with #NotGoingHome. Women talked of their contributions to local ministries. Both women and men honored the female preachers who had inspired their faith or their own calls to ministry. Scripture verses that spoke of women preaching were accompanied by the hashtag. Photos of women who have preached throughout history were posted. A swarm of support for women clergy overtook social media.

Methodist women have sought to argue that the pulpit is their home. They set out to make the public, political, and religious world more homelike. Methodist women, historically and today, pushed the envelope and used their Methodist faith as justification for doing so. They fought for the right to vote and to be ordained; they fought for civil rights and the equal treatment of African Americans before the law; they fought for their own equal treatment before the law through a constitutional amendment; they fought for full reproductive control of their bodies; and they fought for the right to work, preach, and exist in a world that views them as more than sex objects. And they continue to fight; they continue to preach.

Where each of these chapters concludes is not the end of the story. White women gaining suffrage in 1920 through the ratification of the Nineteenth Amendment was not the end. White women and women of color fought to see the passage of the Voting Rights Act in 1965, an act that ensured that state and local governments could no longer employ discriminatory voting practices, such as literacy tests, which prevented mostly African Americans from voting. Through their witness and involvement in the Woman's Division and other Methodist organizations (Board of Missions, Board of Christian Social Concerns, and the Methodist Student Movement), Methodist women marched for voting rights from Selma, Alabama, to Montgomery.[2] In the last

---

2   United Methodist Women, "Voters Rights Toolkit: Protecting Voting Rights," 2016, https://www.unitedmethodistwomen.org/news/votersrightstoolkit.pdf. For a Methodist understanding of the Voting Rights Act, see United Methodist Women, "Resistance to Voter Suppression Still Necessary on the 50th Anniversary of the Voting Rights Act," August 21, 2015, https://www.unitedmethodistwomen.org/news /resistance-to-voter-suppression-still-necessary. For stories on Methodist involvement in the voting rights movement of the 1960s, see Alice Knotts, *Fellowship of Love: Methodist Women Changing American Racial Attitudes, 1920–1968* (Nashville: Kingswood Books, 1996); and Sara M. Evans, *Journeys That Opened up the World: Women, Student Christian Movements, and Social Justice, 1955–1975* (New Brunswick, NJ: Rutgers Univ. Press, 2003).

ten years, the Voting Rights Act has, again, come under attack, and minority groups have been targeted. Their right to access the ballot has been threatened. Rev. Dr. Susan Henry Crowe, general secretary of the General Board of Church and Society of The United Methodist Church, claims that "voting is a matter of faith, citizenship, and democracy." Voting, for her, "is a kind of prayer and faithful testament to the belief that every citizen bears a responsibility and equal right to determine the future of governance in society." Raised United Methodist, she recalls that her family and her faith instilled in her "the value of making the world better through voting."[3] This is reiterated in the *Book of Discipline*, which states that The United Methodist Church "hold[s] governments responsible for the protection of the rights of people to free and fair elections," with a key part of this freedom being the "exercise of the right to vote guaranteed to all adult citizens."[4] Voting is how we, as United Methodists, ensure that social holiness, the overwhelming love of God and neighbor, is spread throughout the systems we've created. It is how we ensure justice and equity. To vote is to act out our Wesleyan faith, a liberative faith that seeks to dismantle injustice. In 2013, a core component of the Voting Rights Act, Section 4, was struck down by a ruling of the Supreme Court of the United States. Before this ruling, states that had previously sought to suppress the votes of minorities (namely, Alabama, Alaska, Arizona, Georgia, Louisiana, Mississippi, South Carolina, Texas, and Virginia) were reviewed by the Justice Department before they could make any change to voting laws.[5] After the ruling, these states were allowed to change their voting laws without review. This has resulted in an increase in voter identification laws, limited polling hours and changed polling locations, restrictions on same-day voter registration, the disenfranchisement of formerly incarcerated individuals, and gerrymandering, all of which limit the fullness and fairness of our electoral system in the United States. In fact, since this ruling, twenty-one states have passed legislation that makes it more difficult for target groups to vote. Henry Crowe sees these actions as "antithetical to the statements of the church and the historic work of United Methodists."[6]

---

3   Susan Henry Crowe, "Voting: A Prayerful Act," *Resource UMC*, accessed December 2, 2019, https://www.resourceumc.org/en/content/voting-a-prayerful-act.

4   *Book of Discipline of The United Methodist Church* (Nashville: United Methodist Publishing House, 2016), ¶164.

5   Shelby County, Alabama v. Holder, Attorney General, et. al. (June 25, 2013), accessed March 9, 2020, https://www.supremecourt.gov/opinions/12pdf/12 -96_6k47.pdf. See also Adam Liptak, "Supreme Court Invalidates Key Part of Voting Rights Act," *New York Times*, June 25, 2013, https://www.nytimes .com/2013/06/26/us/supreme-court-ruling.html

6   Crowe, "Voting."

United Methodist women are still at the forefront of this fight for, nevertheless, they preach suffrage, full suffrage. Gladys Hubbard, a member of Tioga United Methodist Church in Philadelphia and member of the National UMW, presented on voter identification laws within her state of Pennsylvania in 2012. Hubbard was able to garner the full support of the UMW to mobilize behind her on the issue of voter identification laws.[7] Due to Hubbard's campaign, UMW issued an "Action Alert" entitled "Suppression of Voting Rights: A Threat to Democracy," which stated, "A new surge of vote ID laws disproportionately impact seniors, students, and peoples of color. About 11% of eligible Americans (21 million) do not have state-issued photo ids, including 15% of low-income voters, 18% of young eligible voters, 18% of seniors and 25% of African Americans according to The Nation. 13 million adults do not have access to proof of citizenship, which will hinder their efforts to obtain a photo I.D."[8]

UMW used this information to make a call for all United Methodist women to work harder to ensure that people, especially minorities or targeted groups, are registered to vote and have transportation to the polls. UMW also called on these women to check their own states' laws, to ensure that they were registered to vote, and to contact their local and state representative if they believed the laws in their state targeted minorities and prevented them from exercising their right to vote. By 2016, UMW had produced a "Voters Rights Toolkit: Protecting Voting Rights," which outlined what the Voting Rights Act is, the current state of voting rights, who was most at risk for disenfranchisement, and what United Methodist women could do to ensure suffrage for all.[9]

While ensuring that all have equal and legal access to the polls is a modern-day civil rights concern, United Methodist women have continued to support racial equity. In 2012, after the shooting of Trayvon Martin, a new movement began that rightfully and necessarily states that #BlackLivesMatter. Largely begun in response to the unfair and unnecessary killing of black men by police officers, the movement reiterates to the American people how and why racism is built into the very fabric of Americana. It seeks to name racism and white privilege. One United Methodist woman, Diane Johnson, wrote a personal narrative about how and why she joined

7   Peggy Johnson, "ID Laws That Prevent People from Voting in the November Election," August 2012, website of the Eastern Conference of the United Methodist Church, https://www.epaumc.org/archives/news-archive/2012/08/id-laws-that-prevent-people-from-voting-in-the-november-election/.

8   As quoted in Johnson.

9   "Voting Rights Toolkit."

the #BlackLivesMatter movement. She recalls that in 2014, when Michael Brown was shot by police offers, she was just around the corner at a drive-in restaurant. She and her daughter went to go see what had happened and watched as Brown's body lay in the street for four hours. She said, "The day of his death marked the first day of many when people, including myself, took to the streets to demand justice for his death. We kept coming back to protest, for four months."[10]

She wasn't alone. Other United Methodist Women more recently have called on their local schools to observe Black Lives Matter at School Week, a week during the month of February dedicated to the principles of Black Lives Matter. Officially, United Methodist Women as an organization has called for an end to "zero tolerance policies, exclusionary disciplinary policies and practices, and investments in cops rather than school counselors." They also support investment in "Black educators and Black history and ethnic studies curriculum." Harriet Olson, the chief executive officer of UMW, states, "We cannot adhere to our faith without addressing systemic injustice that pushes certain children, namely child of color, out of the classroom and into the criminal justice system. To follow the [tenets] of our faith and live as Jesus taught us we must link arm and arm and support youth of color all across our country who are leading the struggle for racial justice and educational equity."[11] It is because of our faith as United Methodists that we must be continuously fighting for the equity of all before the law.

Fighting for equity before the law includes the continued fight to see the ratification and passage of the Equal Rights Amendment. As recently as 2015, UMW issued an Action Alert calling attention to the continued discrimination of women based on sex across the world. It states:

> It's hard to believe that at a point in history where women hold a record 5.2 percent of CEO jobs at Fortune 500 companies and female representation in our nation's Congress is at its height, women still do not receive equal compensation to men for doing the same job. In fact, American women on average make 78 cents to every dollar made by their male counterparts. That's 22 cents less than a man just because

10 Diane Johnson, "From Civil Rights to Black Lives Matter—A Personal Narrative," United Methodist Women, January 1, 2017, https://www.unitedmethodistwomen .org/news/from-civil-rights-to-black-lives-matter.

11 United Methodist Women, "Help Interrupt School to Prison Pipeline with Black Lives Matter at School Week Action," February 1, 2019, https://www.united methodistwomen.org/news/lay-members-with-umw-organizing-for-black-lives -matter-at-school.

the sex you were born happens to be female. According to the Equal Rights Center, women are 60 percent more likely to have to make a higher down payment on a home than men. These inequities existing as the status quo of our modern society are unacceptable.[12]

United Methodist Women argues that one of the reasons for continued sexist practices, such as unequal pay, are the norms that have been ingrained in our society. We have to combat the norms in order to fully respect women and deem them worthy. One of the fundamental ways of showing respect is to ratify the Equal Rights Amendment, which ensures federally that women are protected from discrimination.

As chapter 4 outlined, United Methodist women have continued to ensure that women have comprehensive health care, including the right to access abortion if necessary. With recent attacks on women's reproductive freedoms through the stream of 2019 abortion bans in states around the country, United Methodist Women decried the acts of legislators who "could hold the lives of girls and women in such low esteem that they would not allow exceptions in cases of rape or incest *and* enact harsher penalties on doctors who performed abortions than on the rapists and incestuous pedophiles."[13] Through UMW and the Board of Church and Society, the UMC has continued to offer trainings and education to women about maternal health, including maternal wellness and mortality programs. At these trainings, women learn how to assess and address the needs of their local communities. Participants visit lawmakers on Capitol Hill, where they have "an opportunity . . . to go and learn what a legislative 'ask' looks like."[14] The hope is that through education and advocacy training, women will go to their local communities, where they'll connect with other coalitions and groups to address the needs of girls and women in their hometowns. These efforts are not new. UMW and its predecessor organizations have always

---

12 United Methodist Women, "'Persons of Equal Stature': Sex Equality and the States," January 9, 2015, https://www.unitedmethodistwomen.org/news/persons-of-equal -stature.

13 United Methodist Women, "United Methodist Women Decries Attack on Women's Reproductive Health," May 17, 2019, accessed 12/1/2019, https://www.united methodistwomen.org/news/united-methodist-women-decries-attack-on-womens -reproductive-health.

14 Erik Alsgaard, "Learning to Advocate for Maternal Health," United Methodist Women, September 2017, https://www.unitedmethodistwomen.org/news/learning-to-advocate -for-maternal-health.

sought to educate women and train them to be local advocates, for never-theless, they preach.

The General Commission on the Status and Role of Women continues to find new ways to address sexual harassment, even addressing the harassment of clergywomen. Since the #ChurchToo movement began in 2017, they have taken new steps and implemented new programs. One of these is a four-session study entitled *The Way of Integrity: Living In Right Relationship with Self, Others, and God.* It provides a "deep exploration of scripture and other resources" where "participants will give intentional attention to core values and the development of self-awareness in all they do."[15] In other words, it hopes to teach people to be more aware of how they act, what they say, and the power they wield and how those elements might affect others. They've also developed a *#MeToo Toolkit*, which brings together various resources of The UMC, including statements from the Social Principles, book discussions, liturgical resources, bulletin inserts, and so on.[16] In consultation with the Council of Bishops, COSROW also issued a press release in January 2018 in response to both #MeToo and #ChurchToo. The members of these groups acknowledge that

> the sin of sexual misconduct must be named by the Church at every level of ministry. Further, we must confront the environment of coarser public dialog and discourse that provides license and cover for sexual harassment, abuse and assault.
>
> We acknowledge that the Church is also a place where sexual misconduct happens when persons in power positions choose to abuse their power. The stories are all too similar. Alleged victims are often reluctant to come forward fearing they will not be believed or they will experience retaliation and the decision to report will be held against them. Sexual misconduct is a symptom of a systemic problem within our Church and society where patriarchy flourishes.[17]

15 General Commission on the Status and Role of Women, *The Way of Integrity: Living in Right Relationship with Self, Others, and God*, accessed December 1, 2019, https://www.gcsrw.org/Portals/13/Curriculum/GCSRW-Integrity%20Project-Leaders'%20Guide_v3-1.pdf?ver=2018-11-15-140147-223.

16 General Commission on the Status and Role of Women, *#MeToo Toolkit*, accessed December 1, 2019, https://www.gcsrw.org/Portals/13/SIte%20Migration/GCSRW-%23METOO%20Toolkit-Online-7.pdf.

17 Council of Bishops of The United Methodist Church, "United Methodist Leaders Respond to #MeToo and #ChurchToo Movement," January 23, 2018, https://nccumc.org/cosrow/files/2018/01/COB-COSROW-JOINT-STATEMENT-JAN-23-18.pdf.

In this statement, the bishops joined COSROW in naming sexual misconduct as a systemic problem in our society, one that must be continuously named in order to be addressed properly. They admit that the church is not innocent when it comes to sexual misconduct, as the church is a place where power dynamics are very real—whether they be clergy over lay or lay over clergy. In probably the most poignant sentence of the press release, the two groups name sexual misconduct as a "symptom of a systemic problem within our Church . . . where patriarchy flourishes." Statements like this need to be made. The church needs to be called out as a place where patriarchy is allowed to and encouraged to flourish on a daily basis. However, these statements need to be followed through with actions that fully support people who report sexual misconduct, support for women in ministry and at all levels of ministry, and encouragement of the use of feminist, queer, and womanist theology that seeks to dismantle patriarchal interpretations of the Christian scriptures.

At the 2016 General Conference of The UMC, Carol Napier, a Sunday school teacher and member of Glenn Memorial United Methodist Church in north Georgia, sought to change the script within United Methodism. She brought a constitutional amendment before the plenary for discussion. It read:

> As the Holy Scripture reveals, both men and women are made in the image of God and, therefore, men and women are of equal value in the eyes of God. The United Methodist Church recognizes it is contrary to Scripture and to logic to say that God is male or female, as maleness and femaleness are characteristics of human bodies and cultures, not characteristics of the divine. The United Methodist Church acknowledges the long history of discrimination against women and girls. The United Methodist Church shall confront and seek to eliminate discrimination against women and girls, whether in organizations or in individuals, in every facet of its life and in society at large. The United Methodist Church shall work collaboratively with others to address concerns that threaten the cause of women's and girls' equality and well-being.[18]

When asked why she had submitted it, Napier responded, "I introduced this constitutional amendment for all the girls around the world who are raised in churches that tell them in subtle and not so subtle ways that they are

---

18 Jessica Brodie, "AC2017 to Vote on Five UMC Constitutional Amendments," South Carolina United Methodist Advocate, March 20, 2017, https://www.advocatesc .org/2017/03/ac2017-to-vote-on-five-umc-constitutional-amendments/.

second-class citizen[s]—and for the women, who have worked so hard to eliminate sexism in the church."[19]

Adding this statement to the constitution of The UMC would have begun the necessary changes to our script, the change needed to fully recognize the dignity and worth of women within our denomination. The first two sentences do that by clearly stating that men and women are made in the image of God and are of equal value in the eyes of God. It then clarified this, again, by saying that God is neither male nor female, for God is divine, not human. The remaining three sentences then clarified even further how a belief that God is male perpetuates discrimination against women and girls and threatens their well-being.

The paragraph was amended on the floor of General Conference. The second sentence was deleted because it was problematic for many United Methodists to admit that God is not in fact male.[20] This is due to the scripts we carry. From the theology that has been handed down to the artwork that hangs in the halls of churches to the weekly references to God as male from pulpits across the world, it is hard for people to fathom that God is not a white-bearded, white-skinned old man. Once the paragraph was amended through the deletion of the second sentence, it was approved by the necessary two-thirds of delegates. Then it was on its way to the annual conferences for ratification.

However, by accident, the unamended paragraph was sent to the annual conferences for ratification, and it was not approved. Many cited the second sentence, which was supposed to have been deleted as the reason why.[21] Unfortunately, this error showed Methodist women that their denomination, which has claimed to be a strong supporter of women's rights and women's ministry, is only willing to have its support go so far. The limit was saying that God is in fact not male. United Methodists, at General Conference and at Annual Conferences, could not admit that. For them, God is male. The error was caught after the votes were made and the results were in: 66.5 percent supported the amendment with the above sentence included, a

---

19 Heather Hahn, "Church Ratifies Women's Equality Amendment," November 6, 2019, UM News, https://www.umnews.org/en/news/church-ratifies-womens-equality -amendment?fbclid=IwAR1f1DZxtqVzQC-bO9LcmO_xBspeUiVUxxgaezYeKSOTxUN wfDPvQ_xHZge.

20 Brodie, "AC2017 to Vote on Five."

21 Kathy L. Gilbert, "Error Forces Revote on Failed Constitutional Amendment," UM News, March 11, 2018, https://www.umnews.org/en/news/error-forces-revote-on -failed-constitutional-amendment.

mere 0.2 percent less than needed to ratify.[22] After the failure was made public, #NeverthelessShePreached surfaced on social media as a way to show the resiliency of women clergy. Despite the continued unwillingness of the church to fully recognize their dignity, worth, and authority, women still preach.

After the failed vote, the correct and amended paragraph was sent back around to the annual conferences, with the "problematic" sentence removed. Results of the corrected and amended constitutional amendment were announced in November 2019. With the sentence stating that God was neither male nor female removed, 92.2 percent of the annual conferences approved of adding it to the constitution.[23] The new paragraph will read:

> As the Holy Scripture reveals, both men and women are made in the image of God and, therefore, men and women are of equal value in the eyes of God. The United Methodist Church acknowledges the long history of discrimination against women and girls. The United Methodist Church shall confront and seek to eliminate discrimination against women and girls, whether in organizations or in individuals, in every facet of its life and in society at large. The United Methodist Church shall work collaboratively with others to address concerns that threaten women's and girls' equality and well-being.[24]

A bittersweet moment. The UMC is willing to say that men and women are both made in the image of God and are of equal value in God's eyes. This is truly remarkable and a necessary step forward in changing our script. However, the idea that The UMC isn't willing to say that God isn't male is still quite problematic.

When the vote was announced, Bishop Tracy Smith Malone, who currently serves as president of COSROW and bishop of the East Ohio Annual Conference, said, "While we still have much progress to make, this is an indication that we as a church do acknowledge and embrace women at every level of the church." Through failed amendments, revotes, celebrations, work yet to be accomplished, and scripts that still need to be changed,

---

22 Results of Annual Conferences Votes on Five Constitutional Amendments, May 7, 2018, http://s3.amazonaws.com/Website_Properties/council-of-bishops/documents/Detailed_results_of_Annual_Conference_Votes_on_Constitutional_Amendments.pdf.

23 Hahn, "Church Ratifies Women's Equality Amendment."

24 Hahn.

nevertheless, they preached. We still have work to do. We still have books to read, sermons to write, missions to serve, people to unite. Even though this book begins with the nineteenth-century efforts of Methodist women to find their voice in the pulpit and in the ballot box, these fights did not begin then. Women have been fighting to have a voice for millennia, and many have found creative ways to have their voices heard. Our fight is not over. I have the utmost confidence that whatever the next obstacle may be, nevertheless, we'll preach.

SELECTED BIBLIOGRAPHY

Anthony, Susan B., and Ida Husted Harper. *A History of Woman Suffrage, 1883–1900*. N.p.: Fowler & Wells, 1902.

The Association of Religion Data Archives. "Can Women Be Religious Leaders?" Accessed February 20, 2020. http://www.thearda.com/ConQS /qs_250.asp.

———. "Can Women Preach?" Accessed February 20, 2020. http://www .thearda.com/ConQS/qs_249.asp.

———. "Gender of Religious Leader." Accessed February 20, 2020. http:// www.thearda.com/ConQS/qs_236.asp.

Blue, Ellen. *Women United for Change: 150 Years in Mission*. New York: United Methodist Women, 2019.

Book of Discipline of The United Methodist Church. Nashville: United Methodist Publishing House, 2016.

Book of Resolutions of The United Methodist Church. Nashville: United Methodist Publishing House, 1970; 1976.

Bordin, Ruth. *Frances Willard: A Biography*. Chapel Hill, NC: Univ. of North Carolina Press, 1986.

Brodie, Jessica. "AC2017 to Vote on Five UMC Constitutional Amendments." March 20, 2017. https://www.advocatesc.org/2017/03/ac2017-to-vote -on-five-umc-constitutional-amendments/.

Cooper, Beth. *Under the Stained Glass Ceiling: Sexual Harassment of United Methodist Clergywomen*. San Diego: Frontrowliving Press, 2011.

Council of Bishops of The United Methodist Church. "United Methodist Leaders Respond to #MeToo and #ChurchToo Movement." January 23, 2018.

Crowe, Susan Henry. "Voting: A Prayerful Act." *Resource UMC.* Accessed December 2, 2019. https://www.resourceumc.org/en/content/voting-a -prayerful-act.

D'Emilio, John, and Estelle B. Freedman, *Intimate Matters: A History of Sexuality in America*, 3rd ed. Chicago: Univ. of Chicago Press, 2012.

Dirks, Doris Andrea, and Patricia A. Relf. *To Offer Compassion: A History of the Clergy Consultation Service on Abortion*. Madison: Univ. of Wisconsin Press, 2019.

Ferreri, Eric. "Study: Female Church Leaders Face Stained-Glass Ceiling," December 9, 2015. The data collected from the study can be found at http://www.soc.duke.edu/natcong/explore.html.

Fiske, Edward B. "Clergymen Offer Abortion Advice." *New York Times*. May 22, 1967. https://www.nytimes.com/1967/05/22/archives/clergymen -offer-abortion-advice-21-ministers-and-rabbis-form-new.html.

Franzen, Trisha. *Anna Howard Shaw: The Work of Woman Suffrage.* Chicago: Univ. of Illinois Press, 2014.

General Commission on the Status and Role of Women. *#MeToo Toolkit.* Accessed December 1, 2019. https://www.gcsrw.org/Portals/13 /SIte%20Migration/GCSRW-%23METOO%20Toolkit-Online-7.pdf.

———. "Gender in the UMC." 2019.

———. "Sexual Misconduct in The United Methodist Church: US Update." Summer 2017.

———. *The Way of Integrity: Living in Right Relationship with Self, Others, and God.* Accessed December 1, 2019. https://www.gcsrw.org /Portals/13/Curriculum/GCSRW-Integrity%20Project-Leaders'%20 Guide_v3-1.pdf?ver=2018-11-15-140147-223.

———. "Women by the Numbers." 2014.

Gifford, Carolyn De Swarte, ed. *Writing Out My Heart: Selections from the Journal of Frances E. Willard, 1855–96.* Chicago: Univ. of Illinois Press, 1995.

Gifford, Carolyn De Swarte, and Amy R. Slagell, eds. *Let Something Good Be Said: Speeches and Writings of Frances E. Willard.* Chicago: Univ. of Illinois Press, 2007.

Gilbert, Kathy L. "Error Forces Revote on Failed Constitutional Amendment." March 11, 2018. https://www.umnews.org/en/news/error-forces-revote -on-failed-constitutional-amendment.

————. "5 Conferences Join Faith Coalition on Reproductive Rights, Abortion." United Methodist News Service. June 22, 2016. https://www.umnews.org/en/news/oregon-idaho-takes-up-support-for-rcrc-denied-at-gc2016.

Gilbert, Sophie. "The Movement of #MeToo: How a Hashtag Got Its Power," October 16, 2017, replicated in "#MeToo Movement: Sexual Hierarchy and Abuse (2016-2018)." Chapter 15 in Micah Issitt. *Opinions throughout History: Gender: Roles & Rights*. Amenia, NY: Grey House, 2018.

Goodrich, Leigh. "Paragraph 4, Article 4 Breakdown." General Commission on the Status and Role of Women. Accessed February 18, 2020, https://gcsrw.org/MonitoringHistory/WomenByTheNumbers/tabid/891/post/paragraph-4-article-4-vote-breakdown/Default.aspx.

Gordon, Mara, and Alyson Hurt. "Early Abortion Bans: Which States Have Passed Them?" *National Public Radio*. June 5, 2019. https://www.npr.org/sections/health-shots/2019/06/05/729753903/early-abortion-bans-which-states-have-passed-them.

Griffith, R. Marie. *Moral Combat: How Sex Divided American Christians and Fractured American Politics*. New York: Basic Books, 2017.

Guttmacher Institute. "An Overview of Abortion Laws." Accessed December 1, 2019. https://www.guttmacher.org/state-policy/explore/overview-abortion-laws.

Hahn, Heather. "Church Ratifies Women's Equality Amendment." November 6, 2019. https://www.umnews.org/en/news/church-ratifies-womens-equality-amendment?fbclid=IwAR1f1DZxtqVzQC-bO9LcmO_xBspeUiVUxxgaezYeKS0TxUNwfDPvQ_xHZge.

————. "5 Constitutional Amendments Head to Vote." United Methodist News Service. February 8, 2017. https://www.umnews.org/en/news/5-constitutional-amendments-head-to-vote.

Harkness, Georgia. *Women in Church and Society*. Nashville: Abingdon Press, 1972.

Heitzenrater, Richard P. *Wesley and the People Called Methodist*, 2nd ed. Nashville: Abingdon Press, 2013.

Johnson, Diane. "From Civil Rights to Black Lives Matter—A Personal Narrative." United Methodist Women. January 1, 2017. https://www.unitedmethodistwomen.org/news/from-civil-rights-to-black-lives-matter.

Johnson, Peggy. "ID Laws That Prevent People from Voting in the November Election." August 2012. https://www.epaumc.org/archives/news-archive/2012/08/id-laws-that-prevent-people-from-voting-in-the-november-election/.

Joy, Emily. "ChurchToo." *Emily Joy Poet* (blog). Accessed December 1, 2019. http://emilyjoypoetry.com/churchtoo.

Kirby, Ellen. *The Evolution of a Focus: Women's Concerns in the Women's Division, 1970–1980*. New York: Women's Division, 1983.

Knotts, Alice. *Fellowship of Love: Methodist Women Changing American Racial Attitudes, 1920–1968*. Nashville: Kingswood Books, 1996.

Lifewatch. "The Durham Declaration." Accessed February 17, 2020. https://www.lifewatch.org/the-durham-declaration.html.

Magalis, Elaine. *Conduct Becoming to a Woman: Bolted Doors and Burgeoning Missions*. Women's Division, Board of Global Ministries, The United Methodist Church, 1973.

Nash, Elizabeth, Lizamarie Mohammed, Olivia Cappello, Sophia Naide, and Zohra Ansari-Thomas. "State Policy Trends at Mid-Year 2019: States Race to Ban or Protect Abortion." Guttmacher Institute. July 1, 2019. https://www.guttmacher.org/article/2019/07/state-policy-trends-mid-year-2019-states-race-ban-or-protect-abortion.

Newman, Louise Rachel. *White Women's Rights: The Racial Origins of Feminism in the United States*. New York: Oxford Univ. Press, 1999.

NC Conference of The UMC. "Women in Ministry." June 2019. https://vimeo.com/335862568.

Outler, Albert, ed. *John Wesley's Sermons: An Anthology*. Nashville: Abingdon Press, 1991.

Pellauer, Mary D. *Toward a Tradition of Feminist Theology: The Religious Social Thought of Elizabeth Cady Stanton, Susan. B. Anthony, and Anna Howard Shaw*. Brooklyn: Carlson, 1991.

"Results of Annual Conferences Votes on Five Constitutional Amendments." May 7, 2018. http://s3.amazonaws.com/Website_Properties/council-of-bishops/documents/Detailed_results_of_Annual_Conference_Votes_on_Constitutional_Amendments.pdf.

Rieger, Joerg. *No Religion but Social Religion: Liberating Wesleyan Theology*. Nashville: Wesley's Foundery Books, 2018.

Shaw, Anna Howard. *The Story of a Pioneer*. Project Gutenberg Ebook. 2008. http://www.gutenberg.org/files/354/354-h/354-h.htm#link2H_4_0009.

Smietana, Bob. "Accusing SBC of 'Caving,' John MacArthur Says of Beth Moore: 'Go Home.'" Religion News Service. October 19, 2019. https://religionnews.com/2019/10/19/accusing-sbc-of-caving-john-macarthur-says-beth-moore-should-go-home/.

Stevens, Thelma. *Legacy for the Future: The History of Christian Social Relations in the Woman's Division of Christian Service, 1940–1968*.

Women's Division, Board of Global Ministries, The United Methodist Church, 1978.

Sullins, Paul. "The Stained Glass Ceiling: Career Attainment for Women Clergy." *Sociology of Religion* 61, no. 3 (Autumn, 2000): 243–66.

United Methodist Insight. "What Do We Really Need to Know? Clergy-woman's Complaint Finds Gaps between Process and Justice." June 8, 2017. https://um-insight.net/in-the-church/ordained-ministry/what-do-we-really-need-to-know/.

United Methodist Women. "The Church Still Supports Women's Reproductive Health, but We Have Work to Do." Accessed December 1, 2019. https://www.unitedmethodistwomen.org/news/the-church-still-supports-womens-reproductive-health.

———. "Help Interrupt School to Prison Pipeline with Black Lives Matter at School Week Action." February 1, 2019. https://www.united methodistwomen.org/news/lay-members-with-umw-organizing-for-black-lives-matter-at-school.

———. "'Persons of Equal Stature': Sex Equality and the States." January 9, 2015. https://www.unitedmethodistwomen.org/news/persons-of-equal-stature.

———. "Resistance to Voter Suppression Still Necessary on the 50th Anniversary of the Voting Rights Act." August 21, 2015. https://www.unitedmethodistwomen.org/news/resistance-to-voter-suppression-still-necessary.

———. "United Methodist Women Decries Attack on Women's Reproductive Health." May 17, 2019. https://www.unitedmethodistwomen.org/news/united-methodist-women-decries-attack-on-womens-reproductive-health.

United Methodist Women. "Voters Rights Toolkit." 2016. https://www.united methodistwomen.org/news/votersrightstoolkit.pdf.

Wang, Amy B. "'Nevertheless, She Persisted' Becomes New Cry After McConnell Silences Elizabeth Warren." *Washington Post*. February 8, 2017.

Wesley, John. "Thoughts on the Present Scarcity of Provisions." London: R. Hawes, 1773.

———. *Preface to Hymns and Poems*. 1739. In *The Works of the Reverend John Wesley, A. M.* Vol. 7. New York: J. Emory and B. Waugh, for the Methodist Episcopal Church, 1831.

Williams, Daniel K. *Defenders of the Unborn: The Pro-Life Movement before Roe v. Wade*. New York: Oxford Univ. Press, 2019.

Archival Records from the General Commission on Archives and History of The United Methodist Church

Administrative Files of United Methodist Communications

"How and Why to Ratify the Equal Rights Amendment." From UMW Asked to Support Proposed Equal Rights Amendment, February 13, 1973.
"Night Letter." From UMW Asked to Support Proposed Equal Rights Amendment, February 13, 1973.
"United Methodist Information." From UMW Asked to Support Equal Rights Amendment, February 13. 1973.
"Women's Division Endorses Equal Rights Amendment." From UMW Asked to Support Proposed Equal Rights Amendment, February 17, 1971.

Administrative Records of the General Commission on the Status and Role of Women

"Equal Rights of Women." From Equal Rights Amendment, Records of the General Commission on the Status and Role of Women, 1976.
Kirby, Ellen. "ERA: For the Sake of the Family." From Equal Rights Amendment, 1976.
Petty, Charles V. "ERA and Family Life," Board of Church and Society, GCAH 2218-4-5-28: ERA 1977.

Administrative Records of the Division of General Welfare of the General Board of Church and Society

Abortion: A Human Choice. Board of Christian Social Concerns of The United Methodist Church, May 1971. "Abortion Packet 1972."
"Why a Religious Committee for the Equal Rights Amendment?" From Involvement with RCERA (Religious Coalition for the Equal Rights Amendment), 1975–1976.

Records of the Women's Division of the General Board of Global Ministries

"Statement of the Religious Coalition for Abortion Rights before the Subcommittee on Civil and Constitutional Rights of the Committee of the Judiciary U.S. House of Representatives" (March 24, 1976). From Religious Coalition for Abortion Rights, 1979.